The Best of

THE
PUBLIC
SQUARE

*Selections from
Richard John Neuhaus'
celebrated column in
First Things*

RPL
New York, New York

ISBN 0-9659507-0-0

Library of Congress Catalog Card Number: 97-74385

02   01   00   99   98   97

10   9   8   7   6   5   4   3   2   1

TABLE OF CONTENTS

INTRODUCTION

Modesty rightly forbids editors from praising their own magazines. The self-bestowed pat on the back, even when deserved, risks breeding that self-satisfied and complacent repetition which is the invariable destruction of good journalism. As the associate editor of FIRST THINGS, I am thus prevented from telling you about the extraordinary success of the magazine since its launching in March 1990. Nor can I mention its astoundingly loyal readers, who seem to think of the magazine's writers and editors as honorary members of their families. I can't even discuss the excitement FIRST THINGS continues to generate in the world of intellectual journalism: publishing in May 1994 the historic joint statement "Catholics and Evangelicals Together"; printing in May 1995 the definitive analysis of the disastrous confrontation between the FBI and the Branch Davidians in Waco; bringing together in November 1996 some of America's most thoughtful philosophers of law to contemplate the role of the judiciary and the possible end of democracy.

I can, however, tell you about FIRST THINGS' most popular feature, the continuing survey of religion and public life that goes by the title of The Public Square and appears each month at the end of the magazine. Written by Father Richard John Neuhaus, the journal's editor-in-chief, The Public Square is one of those rare columns that demand the attention of America's most influential journalists, opinion-makers, and intellectuals—who find it sometimes compelling, sometimes infuriating, but always mandatory reading. But The Public Square is also one of those even rarer columns that manage to inform and excite its general readers—who appreciate its serious discussions of religious and social topics, its lively prose, and its occasional dash of almost wicked humor.

As a Lutheran clergyman, Richard John Neuhaus was for seventeen years senior pastor of a low-income African American parish in Brooklyn, New York, playing a leading role in organizations dealing with civil rights, international justice, and ecumenism. The recipient of numerous awards, he has held presidential appointments in the Carter, Reagan, and Bush administrations and was named by *U.S. News & World Report* as one of the 32 "most influential intellectuals in America." In September 1991 he was ordained a Roman Catholic priest of the Archdiocese of New York. His widely regarded books include *Freedom For Ministry* (1979), *The Naked Public Square: Religion and Democracy in America* (1984), and *The Catholic Moment* (1987).

Those who have never read The Public Square and FIRST THINGS are in for a treat with this anthology, *The Best of The Public Square*. Long-time readers as well will find some of their old friends in this selection from 1990 to 1995. Reading through the back issues of the first five years of his column, Father Neuhaus suggested many of the selected pieces, while the journal's editor, James Nuechterlein, and managing editor, Matthew Berke, insisted upon the inclusion of some of their own favorites. A student from Fordham University, Gregory M. Eirich—the summer intern who deserves great thanks for his help in preparing this anthology—argued the necessity for including so many different pieces that an early draft of the book seemed to reach a thousand pages. I had at last to take a firm line with all my colleagues and reduce the selection to the slim but, I think, representative volume you have in your hands, collecting the pieces into five chapters each approximating the length and range of a typical issue's printing of The Public Square.

Many readers find The Public Square a taste that, once acquired, cannot be lost. If after finishing this anthology you too discover yourself hooked, I am afraid that your only hope is to call 1-800-783-4903 or write P.O. Box 3000, Dept, FT, Denville, NJ 07834 and join FIRST THINGS' growing thousands of subscribers in following month by month Father Neuhaus' continuing survey of religion and public life—along with the other essays and reviews of the many brilliant and influential authors featured in the magazine. An editor's proper modesty forbids me to tell you how much I think you will enjoy it.

—J. Bottum
New York City
July 2, 1997

A POPE OF THE FIRST MILLENNIUM AT THE THRESHOLD OF THE THIRD

Hardly had heads stopped shaking in the publishing world over the astonishing sales of the new *Catechism of the Catholic Church* in the United States (some three million copies in the first few months) than along comes *Crossing the Threshold of Hope*. Knopf put out more than eight million dollars for the American rights and pinned its promotional hopes on the Pope's planned visit to this country in October. When the trip was postponed to next year, executives at Knopf heard the sickening sound of millions of dollars going down the drain. In happy fact, however, *Crossing* immediately jumped to the top of the best-seller lists, with bookstores complaining that they couldn't get enough to meet the demand. It is now expected that the book will earn upward of fifty million dollars worldwide, all of it to be given to church-related charities.

There is something funny going on here if you believe the prestige press, what we have in this book are disjointed philosophical and theological ramblings by a reactionary old man who heads an authoritarian institution that is lamentably out of touch with most Catholics and the entirety of the modern world. Insight into what is going on here begins with not believing the prestige press. Another way of understanding what is happening is proposed by the book's author: "We find ourselves faced with a new reality. The world, tired of ideology, is opening itself to the truth. The time has come when the splendor of this truth (*veritatis splendor*) has begun anew to illuminate the darkness of human existence." Some may think that excessively sanguine. The Pope's hopefulness, however, is in no way to be confused with optimism. Optimism is merely a matter of optics, of seeing what you want to see and not seeing what you don't want to see. The hope in *Crossing the Threshold of Hope* is on the far side of a relentlessly realistic, indeed painfully bleak, understanding of the human circumstance. Which is to say that it is on the far side of the cross.

On the dust jacket, written in the Pope's hand, is "Be not afraid!" This, he notes, was the repeated greeting of the Risen Lord to his disciples. (Here and elsewhere, one is struck by the vibrant employment of numerous biblical passages, making the book, among many other things, an intriguing study in the ecclesial interpretation of Scripture.) "Be not afraid!" is the abiding message of the Church to the world, as it was also the theme of Karol Wojtyla's sermon upon being inaugurated as Pope John Paul II in 1978. The plea of the book, reflected in the title, is that we must not stop at the threshold of hope and faith and love. Be not afraid to cross the threshold, for Christ, having gone ahead, is waiting to receive us on the far side of our fears. The book is philosophical and theological, to be sure, but most of all it is a testament to a profound piety forged in pastoral experience and prayer.

An Open-Ended Conversation

Some pages more than others, but every page evinces the intelligence, the warmth, and the passion of an extraordinary Christian soul. I read this book within days of having had a long and very lively dinner with the Holy Father, and all that we talked about has been much on my mind as I have gone back again and again to *Crossing the Threshold of Hope*. The best way I can describe the book is to say that it is very much like continuing an amiably earnest conversation over the dinner table for another ten or fifteen hours. It's not exactly *Everything You Wanted to Ask the Pope But Never Had the Chance*. It's better than that. There is a great deal that one might never have thought to ask but is essential to know if we are to understand this remarkable man and the faith that he proposes to us and to the world.

As most everybody knows, the genesis of the book was a plan to do an unprecedented worldwide television interview in October 1993, marking the fifteenth year of this pontificate. The interview didn't come off, but the Pope was much taken with the questions submitted by the scheduled interviewer, Vittorio Messori, a noted Italian journalist. And so, in moments snatched between innumerable obligations, John Paul began writing down his responses to the questions, and, if you keep writing things down that way, pretty soon you have what could very well be a book. At least the Pope thought so, and Joaquin Navarro-Valls, the Holy See's press director, thought so, and Leonardo Mondadori of the Mondadori publishing empire thought so, and now it seems that pretty much the whole world agrees.

Promotional hype to the contrary, it is not "unprecedented" for a Pope to publish a personal book that has no official standing. In the last sixteen years, this Pope has published several such books that have received little public attention. The new thing here is that he is responding directly to questions posed by a journalist, and they are questions of great interest to the general public. Another difference is the enormous financial investment that publishers have made in the book, combined, perhaps, with the reality of a world "opening itself to the truth." And, of course, while the book itself has no official status, it does provide invaluable insight into the thinking behind the many encyclicals, apostolic exhortations, and other official documents issuing from this pontificate.

In this commentary I will but touch on a few aspects of *Crossing* that bear upon matters of general interest, with particular reference to questions of concern to non-Catholics. Throughout the book there is a notable tone of modesty, both about his person and about the office he holds. To be sure, there is no trimming on the claims for the Petrine Ministry, but the accent is on the weakness and limits of Peter, and of the successors of Peter. Everything authentically Catholic, the Pope insists, must be understood Christocentrically, and

Christ must be understood as the defining figure for all of humanity. He recognizes that the person of the Pope and the institution of the papacy is a puzzle and scandal for many. In response he cites Augustine, *Vobis sum episcopus, vobiscum christianus*. (For you I am a bishop; with you I am a Christian.) "On further reflection, *christianus* has far greater significance than *episcopus*, even if the subject is the Bishop of Rome."

Similarly Christocentric is the understanding of the Church. The institution of the Church is entirely at the service of the Gospel. He asserts that "the Church itself is first and foremost a 'movement,' a mission." "It is the mission that begins in God the Father and that, through the Son in the Holy Spirit, continually reaches humanity and shapes it in a new way." Elsewhere he suggests that the Church is a "protest movement," challenging all the principalities and powers opposed to the mission of Christ that is the Church. "What else are the sacraments (all of them!), if not the action of Christ in the Holy Spirit? When the Church baptizes, it is Christ who baptizes; when the Church absolves, it is Christ who absolves; when the Church celebrates the Eucharist, it is Christ who celebrates it: 'This is my body.' . . . All the sacraments are an action of Christ, the action of God in Christ." The foregoing is in response to Messori's observation that people are perplexed by the silence of God. In light of the continuing action of God in Christ, says John Paul, "it is truly difficult to speak of the silence of God. One must speak, rather, of the desire to stifle the voice of God."

Unity of Christians, Unity of Humankind

Repeatedly, the Pope returns to the question of ecumenism, and the connection between Christian unity and the unity of mankind. Those who have followed this pontificate with even moderate attentiveness know that there has never been the slightest question about the priority attached to ecumenism. On this score both traditionalist and progressivist Catholics have yet to catch up with the Pope. Traditionalists hesitate to cross the threshold and embrace ecumenism as an integral component of Catholic orthodoxy, while progressivists shrink back from the assertion that the only unity the Church can desire is unity in the truth. Divisions among Christians are a result of human sin, for sure, but John Paul suggests that something else, Someone else, has a hand in this. "Could it not be that these divisions have also been a path continually leading the Church to discover the untold wealth contained in Christ's Gospel and in the redemption accomplished by Christ? Perhaps all this wealth would not have come to light otherwise."

In this book and elsewhere, John Paul regularly makes reference to what the West has to learn from the Christian East, and it is no secret that the reconciliation of East and West is viewed as the primary ecumenical responsibility of Rome. But his reflections suggest that there is also a deeper understanding of the Gospel issuing from divisions in the West, between Rome and the communities that claim the legacy of the sixteenth-century Reformation. The healing of the breach between Rome and the Reformation requires an appreciation of a "certain dialectic" in how the Holy Spirit leads us into all truth. "It is necessary for humanity to achieve unity through plurality, to learn to come together in the one Church, even while presenting a plurality of ways of thinking and acting, of cultures and civilizations." Divisions, then, may have served a purpose, but that does not justify continuing divisions that do not serve the truth. "The time must come for the love that unites us to be manifested! Many things lead us to believe that that time is now here."

The charge that the Lord Jesus gave to Peter makes ecumenism imperative. "The Petrine ministry is also a ministry of unity," and that is entirely consonant with the Lord's command to Peter, "Strengthen your brothers in faith." John Paul thinks it significant that these words were said just as Peter was about to deny Jesus. "It was as if the Master Himself wanted to tell Peter: 'Remember that you are weak, that you, too, need endless conversion. You are able to strengthen others only insofar as you are aware of your own weakness.'" Since the Second Vatican Council the Catholic Church has spoken many times about sins against Christian unity. But this note of repentance and confession is now struck with increased urgency.

At a consistory of cardinals last May, a draft program was proposed to prepare for the Jubilee Year 2000. The program reportedly emphasized the need for the Church to confess its sins, not only against Christian unity but also in events such as the Inquisition and the persecution of heretics and Jews. It is said the draft was not well received by many cardinals. If the Church is the Body of Christ, some worry, one must be careful in speaking about the Church being capable of sinning. While such cautions are legitimate, it will not do to speak merely about individual members of the Church sinning, as though the authoritative structures and institutions that define the Roman Catholic Church are not implicated in their actions. Some inexcusably bad things have been done by popes and cardinals and bishops and religious orders—all inextricably entangled with what is meant by the "Catholic Church." Beginning with his persistent reference to "the weakness of Peter," this Pope seems to be searching for the appropriate way to ensure that, at the threshold of the Third Millennium, the Church will be found on her knees seeking for herself the for-giveness she declares to others. For Christians and for the world, it is thought, there must be something like an act of universal repentance and absolution if we are to walk upright into the Third Millennium. What such an act (or acts) might be remains unclear, but this Pope clearly intends to be with us in crossing that threshold, and in a November letter he had more to say about how we might cross it more fully united as forgiven sinners. In that letter, John Paul said that the Church must "become more fully conscious of the sinfulness of her children, recalling all those times in history when they depart-ed from the spirit of Christ" and thus "sullied the face [of the Church]."

No Salvation Outside Christ

The concern for Christian unity inevitably comes up against what some view as Rome's exclusivist claims to being, quite simply and without remainder, the Church of Christ. As is evident in a chapter of particular ecumenical interest ("Is Only Rome Right?"), that is not what the Catholic Church claims. "Outside the Church there is no salvation," John Paul suggests, is another way of stating the "revealed truth that there is salvation only and exclusively in Christ." Here he weaves a rich tapestry of biblical texts and the teaching of the Council that "The Church is in Christ as a sacrament, or a sign and instrument, of intimate union with God and of the unity of the entire human race." To be saved is to be brought into the most intimate life of God, "into the Mystery of the Divine Trinity."

This happens in the Church but that "cannot be understood by looking exclusively at the visible aspect of the Church." The Pope does not put it quite this way, but the implication is that, where this incorporation into the life of God happens, where salvation happens, there is the Church. The Church, he says, "is far from proclaiming any kind of ecclesiocentrism. Its teaching is Christocentric in all of its aspects, and therefore it is profoundly rooted in the Mystery of the Trinity." Christ and the Church, one is invited to think, are coterminous. There are various levels and spheres of communion with the Church as it is most fully and rightly expressed in the Roman Catholic Church, but, in the final analysis, to say that there is no salvation outside the Church is another way of saying that there is no salvation outside Christ. This does not mean that only Christians can be saved. As the Pope turns to the question of world religions and the many who are not Christians, it appears that there are many who do not know the name of Christ who nonetheless are not outside Christ.

Asked why there are so many religions, John Paul refers, as he does regularly throughout this book, to the teaching of the Second Vatican Council. The several parts of that teaching must be kept in play. One part is that the "Church rejects nothing that is true and holy in these religions." Because truth and holiness are from God, all the many evidences of truth and holiness are of a piece, for God is one. In other religions can be found *semina Verbi* (seeds of the Word); their doctrines can "reflect a ray of that truth which enlightens all men," that truth being Christ. The Church "is bound to proclaim that Christ is 'the way and the truth and the life.'" Whatever truth and holiness is to be found anywhere finds its fulfillment in Christ, through whom God has reconciled everything to Himself. In considering the many ways of religion in the world, both past and present, we can affirm, says John Paul, that "Christ came into the world for all these peoples. He redeemed them all and has His own ways of reaching each of them in the present eschatological phase of salvation history."

As generous as he obviously wishes to be to all, the Pope offers rather sharp strictures with respect to, for instance, Buddhism and Islam. Buddhism, with its disdain for and detachment from the world, has some similarity to varieties of Christian mysticism, but such Christian mysticism "begins at the point where the reflections of Buddha end." The Christian goal is not nirvana but perfect incorporation into the life of the Triune God. Islam is similarly limited: "Some of the most beautiful names in the human language are given to the God of the Koran, but He is ultimately a God outside of the world, a God who is only Majesty, never Emmanuel, God-with-us. Islam is not a religion of redemption. There is no room for the Cross and the Resurrection. . . . For this reason not only the theology but also the anthropology of Islam is very distant from Christianity."

While the Pope stresses the requirement of respect for what is true and holy in all religions, it is when he comes to Judaism that respect is clearly joined to deep affection. Here are our "elder brothers in the faith," a phrase John Paul has employed innumerable times. In the chapter devoted to Judaism, he recalls childhood experiences in Poland and the unspeakable crimes of the Nazi period. As Pope he has met frequently with Jewish groups, and he was the first Pope to worship at the great synagogue in Rome. At one such meeting a Jewish leader said, "I want to thank the Pope for all that the Catholic Church has done over the last two thousand years to make the true God known." Some Jewish thinkers have suggested that Christianity is Judaism for the Gentiles, the way in which the God of Abraham, Isaac, and Jacob has, through Jesus, extended the covenant to the nations.

While not subscribing to that formulation, John Paul proposes a heightened sense of alertness to the mysterious and continuing bond between Christian and Jew. Israel and the Church are "two great moments of divine election," and they "are drawing closer together." What is said about the unique relationship between Christianity and Judaism does not detract from but is based upon Jesus the Christ as the fulfillment of God's promise. "The New Covenant," says John Paul, "has its roots in the Old. The time when the people of the Old Covenant will be able to see themselves as part of the New is, naturally, a question to be left to the Holy Spirit. We, as human beings, try only not to put obstacles in the way." Twice he notes the significance of the fact that the Church's dialogue with Jews is conducted by the Pontifical Council for Promoting Christian Unity, whereas dialogue with other religions is under different curial auspices. This reflects a recognition that a singular measure of unity already exists between those who worship the God of Abraham, Isaac, Jacob, and Jesus.

John Paul is not much taken with the effluence of religiosities that appear under the banner of New Age. This, he suggests, is but another instance of the return of ancient gnosticism, the idea that liberation from the real world can be achieved by the adepts of a superior "gnosis" or "spiritual consciousness." The Pope observes, "Gnosticism never completely abandoned the realm of Christianity. Instead, it has always existed side by side with Christianity, sometimes taking the shape of a philosophical movement, but more often assuming the characteristics of a religion or para-religion in distinct, if not declared, conflict with all that is essentially Christian." Here and elsewhere, the heart of what is essentially Christian is Christ—the Word of God incarnate, redeeming the human project and drawing it to its completion in the life of the Holy Trinity. In this view, Judaism and Christianity—unlike Buddhism, Islam, and other traditions—understand creation and redemption in historical continuity; the accent of hope is not on salvation from the world but on the salvation of the world. In support, he repeatedly cites John 3:16, "For God so loved the world . . ."

To Keep Conscience on Guard

Speaking of salvation invites reflection on damnation. In some forms of piety to be found among both Protestants and Catholics, salvation is defined almost exclusively by reference to damnation. To be saved is to be snatched from hell, which is the destination of the generality of humankind. This is not the sensibility of John Paul, who, with early fathers of the Church and the continuing tradition of Orthodoxy, emphasizes the cosmic nature of a redemption that is directed toward the fulfillment of man in the life of God, indeed toward *theosis* or deification. Nonetheless the Pope is concerned about preachers and catechists who "no longer have the courage to preach the threat of hell. And perhaps even those who listen to them have stopped being afraid of hell."

He sympathetically recognizes that the undeniably biblical teaching about hell has been a problem for great Christian thinkers from Origen in the third century to Hans Urs von Balthasar in the twentieth. After all, it is clearly God's will that "all should be saved and come to the knowledge of the truth" (1 Timothy 2). Or, as John Paul puts the question, "Can God, who has loved man so much, permit the man who rejects Him to be condemned to eternal torment?" He answers, "And yet, the words of Christ are unequivocal." In Matthew 25, for example, Christ speaks clearly about those who will go to eternal punishment. So who is in hell? "The Church has never made any pronouncement in this regard. This is a mystery, truly inscrutable, which embraces the holiness of God and the conscience of man. The silence of the Church is, therefore, the only appropriate position for Christian faith. Even when Jesus says of Judas, 'It would be better for that man if he had never been born,' His words do not allude for certain to eternal damnation."

It is the case, however, that "there is something in man's moral conscience" that rebels against the loss of the doctrine of hell. After all, the God who is Love is also ultimate Justice. Reflecting on those who are responsible for creating "hells on earth," one must ask: "Can He tolerate these terrible crimes, can they go unpunished? Isn't final punishment in some way necessary in order to reestablish moral equilibrium in the complex history of humanity? Is not hell in a certain sense the ultimate safeguard of man's moral conscience?" Among some Protestants there is considerable anxiety that the Catholic Church teaches "universalism," the doctrine that all will ultimately be saved, or even Pelagianism, the heresy that it is possible to be saved without the grace of God in Christ. John Paul goes to some pains to clarify these questions.

He notes that ancient councils of the Church rejected the theory of a final *apocatastasis* according to which all would finally be saved and hell abolished. Yet one gathers he does not disagree with von Balthasar, who, in a famous essay by that title, asked, "Dare one hope that all will be saved?" The answer would seem to be that one may so hope—perhaps even that one must so hope—while not denying the abiding alternative to salvation, which is damnation. As for Pelagianism, his interviewer asks whether one cannot live "an honest, upright life even without the Gospel." John Paul: "I would respond that if a life is truly upright it is because the Gospel, not known and therefore not rejected on a conscious level, is in reality already at work in the depths of the person who searches for the truth with honest effort and who willingly accepts it as soon as it becomes known to him. Such willingness is, in fact, a manifestation of grace at work in the soul. The spirit blows where He will and as He wills (John 3). The freedom of the Spirit meets the freedom of man and fully confirms it." In sum, there is no salvation apart from the grace of God in Christ. Even those who have never heard of Christ are, if they are saved, saved because of Christ. (For a fuller discussion of these matters see my commentary on *Redemptoris Missio*, the encyclical on Christian missionary work, "Reviving the Missionary Mandate," FIRST THINGS, October 1991.)

Behold the Man!

But this discussion may give the misleading impression

that *Crossing the Threshold of Hope* is an exercise in systematic theology. There is theological reflection, of course, but in the main it is an unabashedly personal disclosure of how this Pope understands himself, his office, the responsibilities of the Church, and, above all, the strange ways of God with man. There is much on his devotion to Mary and why the typology of male and female is essential to understanding Christ and his bride, the Church. Some readers will find the most affecting parts of the book to be the autobiographical reflections, especially on his abiding concern for young people. He says, "As a young priest I learned to love human love." Such human love, rightly ordered, is on a continuum with the love of God, His for us and ours for Him.

This continuum of the life of God and the life of man is at the heart of all of John Paul's thinking. This is the humanism in his "prophetic humanism." He never tires of repeating that the revelation of God in Christ is the revelation of God to man but also the revelation of man to himself Citing Blaise Pascal he says, "Only in transcending himself does man become fully human." (*Apprenez que l'homme passe infiniment l'homme.*) This truth is demonstrated by Christ in his love that is perfectly ordered to the Father in the power of the Spirit. Thus Christ has "touched the intimate truth of man." "He has touched it first of all with His Cross. Pilate, who pointing to the Nazarene crowned with thorns after his scourging said, 'Behold, the man!', did not realize that he was proclaiming an essential truth, expressing that which always and everywhere remains the heart of evangelization."

John Paul is impatient with sociological analyses of spiritual realities. The Church does not march to statistical calculations but to the songs of Zion. At the same time, he does not shrink from offering his own assessment of the Church's circumstance at the edge of the Third Millennium. "If the post-conciliar Church has difficulties in the area of doctrine and discipline, these difficulties are not serious enough to present a real threat of new divisions. The Church of the Second Vatican Council . . . truly serves this world in a variety of ways and presents itself as the true Body of Christ, as the minister of His saving and redemptive mission, as the promoter of justice and peace." As the major transnational community, the Church is a force also in international affairs. "Not everyone is comfortable with this force, but the Church continues to repeat with the Apostles: 'It is impossible for us not to speak about what we have seen and heard' (Acts 4)."

Tom Burns, former editor of the *Tablet* (London), catches the feel of the book very nicely. "To write of John Paul II as a pontiff of the first millennium is not to say that he is an anachronism, but on the contrary that the radicalism of that time, when grace struck its roots into nature, when the blood of the martyrs was the seed of the Church, and mankind had to choose between stark alternatives, has come round full circle. The most modern of all popes recalls the most distant in time: 'Against the spirit of the world, the Church takes up anew each day a struggle that is none other than the struggle for the world's soul. . . . The struggle for the soul of the contemporary world is at its height when the spirit of the world seems strongest'—words that might have been spoken in the catacombs of ancient Rome." At the threshold of the Third Millennium, they are words of invitation to cross the threshold of hope. (*January 1995*)

FT

Pluralism and Wrong Answers

Because the U.S. Census does not ask about religion, we must rely upon other sources to know how Americans identify themselves religiously. Especially valuable in this connection was a nationwide survey conducted by the City University of New York, the results of which are now brought together in *One Nation Under God: Religion in Contemporary American Society* by Barry A. Kosman and Seymour P. Lachman (Harmony). One reason commonly given for the exclusion or muting of religion in our public life is that we are now a "pluralistic society in which it cannot be assumed that, for instance, the Judeo-Christian ethic is broadly shared. The Kosman-Lachman findings make complete hash of that contention, and it is worth noting that their findings are confirmed by Gallup and other studies.

Statistically at least, America is as much a Christian nation as it ever was, and perhaps more so. Of all Americans, 86.2 percent identify themselves as Christian, with all but 14 percent of those claiming to belong to a specific denomination. Jews are 1.8 percent, which is moved up to 2.2 percent if one counts those who say they are cultural or ethnic, but not religious, Jews. All the other religions put together (Muslim, Unitarian, Buddhist, Hindu, Native American, Sikh, etc.) account for 1.5 percent of the population, while 8.2 percent of Americans say they have no religion. According to these studies, there are 1.5 million Muslims, with 40 percent of them being native black Americans.

The allegedly "exploding" Muslim population is frequently cited by those who contend for the religio-cultural balkanization of America. Muslim organizations claim figures as high as seven million, and these claims are often cited in news stories. For perfectly understandable reasons, minority groups tend to inflate their figures, a relatively innocent vice except when it plays into the hands of those with a more dubious agenda. In this case the dubious agenda is to relegate Christian views to a marginal status in public discourse. Of course many Christians are no more than nominal, and of course there is no one view held by Christians on a host of disputed questions, and of course a hundred other important qualifications. But one of the most elementary facts about America is that its people are overwhelmingly Christian in their own understanding, and that they and many who are not Christian assume that the moral baseline of the society is the Judeo-Christian ethic. Acknowledging that does not answer the many questions that vex our public life, but to ignore it is a guaranteed formula for getting the wrong answers. (June/July 1994)

SENSITIVITY AND INSENSIBILITY AT HARVARD

The same issue of the *Harvard Crimson* contains two stories on different developments driven by one principle. The first is that the Civil Liberties Union of Harvard (CLUH, a kind of hard-core ACLU within the ACLU) is pushing for coed rooms. Jolyon A. Silversmith of that organization says that, in assigning student rooms, it shouldn't make any difference that "the friends they want to live with are of the opposite sex." After all, students of the same sex are permitted to room together and, from what one hears of Harvard these days, that is likely to be just as libidinous. Apparently the administration is listening to the CLUH proposal with sensitivity. The second story is that a tutor at Dunster House is pushing to overturn a practice in which one toaster in the house is reserved for kosher use. It is, he claims, an establishment of religion.

Of the proposal that boys and girls should be allowed to room together, CLUH says, "In general we found students' responses to be very positive." The tutor's anti-toaster campaign is meeting with greater resistance. It seems that some students detect something suspiciously anti-Jewish about it, although the tutor pleads innocent, pointing out that he's against all religions. The principle that drives both developments, of course, is that justice requires absolute nondiscrimination. Incidentals such as sex and religion must not be permitted to impinge upon equality of treatment. The Dunster tutor allows that Jews can't help being Jews since they're born that way, "but they choose to eat kosher." The university is thereby, presumably, violating the constitution of the American Way by endorsing their religious choice.

On the coed room campaign, we wonder if CLUH should not examine the problem more carefully. What is this business about respecting the choice of "the friends they want to live with"? Surely nothing could be more discriminatory than selecting some people as friends while not selecting others. A closer look, we cannot help but suspect, would reveal that factors such as "looksism," "ableism," "heterosexism," and "being-a-pleasant-person-to-be-withism" all enter into student decisions about whom they want to room with. The insensitive may dismiss the seriousness of such concerns, but do they know how it feels to be the victim of "selectivism" when you're not chosen by the person you wanted to room with? We expect better of CLUH. Maybe an affirmative program for the victims of selectivism. Better yet, room assignment by lottery.

It's important to be sensitive, but if sensitivity to human particulars gets in the way of justice, sensitivity will just have to go. And those Jewish kids who insist on being Jewish can go live with their own kind. They're lucky that this secular university lets them attend classes. That they want to live with the rest of us is a bit too much. Equality requires that they be equal like us, which means that they be like us. Such is the elevated level of moral discourse in the Craven Old World that is Harvard. For this parents, desperately hoping that their child will be admitted, are eager to pay $30,000 or more per year. There's a Harvard parent born every minute, as Phineas Taylor Barnum did not live to observe. (*August/September 1992*)

FT

THE SCHAEFFER LEGACY

The magazine of the Rutherford Institute devotes an issue to Francis Schaeffer of L'Abri fame and complains that his legacy is being neglected. The importance of Schaeffer on the world Christian scene is exaggerated by some. In the issue of the *Rutherford Journal*, this writer is accused, if that is the right word, of "only now discovering the truths that Francis Schaeffer championed twenty, even thirty, years ago." The author of the article continues, "Yet, strangely, Francis Schaeffer seems to be given little credit for his ground-breaking work." We have on other occasions been asked about the influence of Schaeffer on our thinking, and perhaps a word is owed especially our evangelical Protestant friends, for whom the impact of Schaeffer is indeed great.

If we are accused of cribbing from people—and we make no claims to being terribly original—we would like to plead guilty to going back somewhat farther than twenty or thirty years. To Paul, Origen, Irenaeus, Augustine, Bonaventure, Thomas, Luther, Calvin, Barth, and von Balthasar, for examples. But we can say, truly, that some of our best friends were formed in crucial ways by Francis Schaeffer and his L'Abri community in Switzerland. For many Evangelicals, Schaeffer, an astonishing autodidact, made accessible a large part of the history of Western thought construed according to his distinctive Christian vision. In the evangelical community, his influence was possibly only second, albeit a very distant second, to that of C. S. Lewis.

And so, although we are not aware of being significantly influenced by Schaeffer, it is easy to agree with the Rutherford folk that his contribution was, and is, enormous. At the risk of offending, however, Evangelicals would do well to expand their canon of intellectual saints. The Christian intellectual tradition does not begin with the publication of Lewis' *Mere Christianity* or with the founding of L'Abri in 1954. This is not to detract in any way from the stature of Francis Schaeffer. It is to put him in the larger Christian context where Schaeffer at his best wanted to be.

In the same issue of the *Rutherford Journal*, Mark Noll of Wheaton acknowledges the great good done by Schaeffer, but does not blink the fact that the man had very considerable weaknesses. As is common with autodidacts, he frequently popped off on questions about which he had no conspicuous knowledge. So, notes Noll, he condemned Aquinas, "judging the medieval theologian by standards that came into play, at best, six or seven hundred years after Aquinas lived." A nice touch, perhaps saying a great deal about Evangelicaldom, is that after Noll's reference to Thomas Aquinas the editors make the explanatory insertion, "[an Italian theologian and philosopher]."

Finally, John Whitehead of Rutherford offers a point that bears remembering. "With the publication of Schaeffer's book *Whatever Happened to the Human Race?* in 1978, the entire complexion of Protestant Christianity began to change. Until this point, virtually no one within the evangelical community was even discussing the sanctity of human life, let alone defending it. Abortion was still characterized as a 'Catholic issue.'" For that alone, and that is far from all that he did, Francis Schaeffer deserves to be celebrated with gratitude. (*June/July 1993*)

FT

PSYCHIATRY'S SHRINKING MARKET

The *Diagnostic and Statistical Manual of Mental Disorders* is published by the American Psychiatric Association (APA), and the new edition takes a more sympathetic tack toward religion. The manual includes a new entry titled "Religious and Spiritual Problems" which will be listed along with other problems of living that do not necessarily indicate psychiatric illness but may be "the focus of clinical attention." Changes in the manual occur from time to time, both reflecting and influencing social attitudes and legal practice. The manual also provides a common terminology to justify research and the billing of patients. In 1973, as the result of an enormous political effort by gays, homosexuality was dropped from the manual's list of personality disorders. Twenty years later religion gets equal status with homosexuality; it may be a problem for some but it is not of itself an illness.

Dr. Harold Alan Pincus of the APA's office of research said the new entry on religion is a sign of the profession's growing sensitivity not only to religion but to cultural diversity generally. Illustrating that diversity is Dr. Francis Lu, a San Francisco psychiatrist, who was involved in bringing about the change because of his personal experience. He said that in

1978 he attended a five-day seminar led by Joseph Campbell, the late mythologist, and there he had "a revelation or an epiphany that in some way my purpose in life was to bring together the East and the West." Working for this change in the manual, he explained, "is part of my living out of that epiphany."

It is possible that some religious folk may be pathetically grateful for the measure of acceptance extended by the APA. The more reasonable view is that the collapse of the plausibility of psychiatric orthodoxy, combined with the dramatic loss of market shares to low-cost small group therapies and psychopharmacologies (such as Prozac), compels the APA to desist from egregiously insulting potential customers, including religious customers. The change in the manual says less about a new appreciation of religion than about a profession that is on the ropes both economically and in terms of its credibility (the two being, of course, intimately coupled). Fitting religion in under the increasingly capacious rubric of "cultural diversity" is doing religion no favors. We may want to reciprocate by allowing that psychiatry is not necessarily a disease but it is a life problem that may require spiritual attention. (*May 1994*)

FT

THE SOURCES OF TOLERANCE

James Davison Hunter's *Culture Wars: The Struggle to Define America* (Basic Books) is receiving a good deal of deserved attention. Hunter, an important participant in the program of the Institute on Religion and Public Life, elaborates in careful sociological fashion some of the foundational ideas that brought this journal into being. The most important of those ideas is that politics is in largest part a function of culture, and at the heart of culture is religion (whether it is called religion or not). Thus, as we have said so often, American public life is best understood in terms of a *Kulturkampf*, a battle over the ideas, moralities, stories, and symbols by which we will order our life together. The great merit of Hunter's work is that he has taken those ideas and fleshed them out with sociological theory and very useful data.

One fairly typical reaction to the *Kulturkampf* argument is by Alan Wolfe of New York's New School. Writing in *The New Republic*, Wolfe observes that Americans are peculiar in the way that they invest their public energies in cultural rather than properly political issues. "It is not because Americans are politically sophisticated that they constantly frustrate those who would understand them," he writes, "but because they are politically innocent. Unable to abolish war, they have abolished politics; the state has not withered away, but the amount of attention paid to its affairs has withered badly." In what Hunter describes as a war between cosmologies—with secular modernists on the one side and orthodox believers on the other—Wolfe is beyond doubt on the modernist side. He admires the way that Hunter "remains neutral" in his analysis of the war, but he finally thinks such neutrality impossible.

Wolfe writes: "Nowhere is the difference between these worldviews clearer than in the fundamentalist assumption, cited numerous times throughout Hunter's book, that we are a Christian nation. At the risk of seeming intolerant of those who hold this position, we are not. There are Jews, Muslims, and any number of other non-Christians who live here and claim the rights of citizens. Fundamentalist language excludes them; liberal modernist language includes them. This is the reason, finally, that Hunter's evenhandedness fails: only one side in this war can live with the other. And the other side cannot reciprocate the respect."

The liberal modernist, says Wolfe, is willing to grant the "fundamentalist" the right to dissent, just so long as religion doesn't get in the way of the liberal ordering of society. At the heart of that order is the axiom of "faith in private and toleration in public"—i.e., the naked public square. Wolfe, and so many of like mind, just don't get it. Their notion of compromise is, "Let's compromise; we'll do it our way." Their notion of tolerance is, "We'll tolerate you so long as you don't trouble us with your different ideas." Some compromise. Some tolerance.

The simplistic worldview espoused by Wolfe is apparently impervious to the fact that even his liberal tolerance cannot stand on its own feet. He repeatedly adverts to democratic "process" and "procedure" as though the style of public discourse he favors is self-evidently right and therefore requires no justification. He does not offer an argument, he simply states a prejudice. The prejudice is most specifically against religion in public. "In a nation composed of people with diverse religious beliefs, no single religion can provide the moral framework for a public vocabulary," he writes. If a "single religion" can mean the Judeo-Christian tradition broadly construed, the assertion is obviously false. That tradition does provide the public vocabulary. Historically and at present, it also provides the way of including other vocabularies, such as that of ancient Athens and even of the secular liberalism that Wolfe favors.

In a magazine as sophisticated as *The New Republic* sometimes is, it is remarkable to find the tired complaint about this not being "a Christian nation." Of course this is not a Christian nation in the way that the Puritans intended the Bay Colony to be a Christian commonwealth. Our public life is manifestly not characterized by Christian virtues. But demographically and culturally it is equally obvious that this is a Christian nation. Nearly 90 percent of the American people claim to be Christians. Unless Mr. Wolfe is prepared to impose a theological or moral test for "true Christianity," it seems rather willful of him to deny that these people are Christians.

Would the Wolfes of our secularized elites deny any other generalization about this society that was borne out in the case of 90 percent of the population? How about the assertion that America is an English-speaking nation? It seems very doubtful that Mr. Wolfe would respond to that assertion by writing, "At the risk of seeming intolerant to those who hold this position, we are not. There are Spanish-speakers, and Chinese-speakers, and the speakers of any number of other languages who live here and claim the rights of citizens." America is Christian in the way that it is English-speaking. Relatively few speak the language very well, there is little agreement on how it should be spoken, some speak it hardly at all, but they all live here and claim the rights of citizens.

What James Hunter obviously has not gotten Alan Wolfe to understand is that the overwhelming majority of Americans derive their moral vocabulary and moral judgments, directly or indirectly, from religion. Whether we like that or not, it is the social fact. And the religion in question is overwhelmingly Christian of a sort that is comfortable in affirming a Judeo-Christian tradition. In private and in public, most Americans speak Christian—although when speaking in public many of them think it is their Christian duty (or a constitutional requirement) that they pretend that they are not speaking Christian. The secular dogma, propounded by Wolfe and many others, that religion must be contained entirely in the private sphere only encourages the pretense. The result, ironically, is that many Americans are discouraged from making in public the religiously grounded moral arguments for tolerating liberal secularists such as Alan Wolfe. (*January 1992*)

FT

NEVER AGAIN?

For most people in the West it is possibly the case that the only absolutely unambiguous icon of evil is the Third Reich and the Holocaust. One may argue that there are other instances of evil that should have that status in the popular consciousness, but they don't. It is therefore understandable that we continue to make moral discernments by employing Nazism as an absolute test line separating the discussible from the unspeakable. A new book from Oxford represents such an exercise in discernment, Stefan Kühl's *The Nazi Connection: Eugenics, American Racism, and German National Socialism*. It is a short (160 pp.), assiduously documented, and devastating account of the way in which American scientists admired and abetted Nazi schemes of racial eugenics in the 1930s, and how they changed their stories and tried to cover their tracks after 1945 when the full dimensions of the Nazi horror became more widely known.

Kühl's is a necessary reminder of how very liberal and progressive the advocacy of eugenics was thought to be in the first half of this century. Negative eugenics, the elimination of the "unfit," and positive eugenics, the breeding of "superior stock," were both greatly favored by the enlightened of the day. Even before the Nazis came to power, German scientists and politicians declared their indebtedness to the inspiring example of America's pioneering programs of sterilizing the mentally deficient and criminally prone. The American example is favorably cited in Hitler's *Mein Kampf* and in the 1930s he wrote admiring letters to prominent American scientists who fully reciprocated his sentiments. Oliver Wendell Holmes had written in a notorious court decision that "three generations of imbeciles is enough," and it was this "realistic" approach of the Americans that German writers lifted up in unfavorable contrast to what they criticized as the dilatory ways of German scientists and policy makers. Come the Third Reich and the world would learn the new meaning of realism.

The leaders of some of the most distinguished universities and research institutions in America were ardently courted by the Nazis. The 550th anniversary of the University of Heidelberg in 1936 was marked by the bestowing of honorary doctorates on prominent American eugenicists, including Foster Kennedy, a psychiatrist and major figure in the Euthanasia Society of the United States until he broke with the society because it was squeamish about advocating the involuntary and systematic extermination of the mentally and physically unfit. In the eyes of a good many American scientists, the Germans would become the model of a rational determination that refused to be inhibited by sentimental concern for the weak who were allegedly jeopardizing the future of the race.

As useful as Kühl's study is, there are disappointing omissions and moments of curious reticence. One suspects that Kühl, a German academic, was too well coached by some of the American advisers whom he thanks in his introduction. In any event, he steers clear of the turbulent waters surrounding some of the contemporary questions most pertinent to his subject. By organizing his interpretation around scientists and "American racism," he severely narrows the focus to include chiefly those scientists who espoused theories that today we would call racist. When it comes to commenting on the contemporary significance of his story, this leaves him with a handful of villains on the kooky margins of scientific and political discourse. His own account makes it clear, however, that most of the American scientists and public policy experts involved were too savvy to make an explicitly racialist argument for eugenics. While racial overtones were almost everywhere present, the formal advocacy was usually framed in terms of the fitness or unfitness not of racial groups but of individuals.

Then too, there is no attention paid the campaign for birth and population control during the period studied. Margaret Sanger, the patron saint of Planned Parenthood, is not mentioned even once, although her views (often explicitly racial) closely paralleled those of the eugenicists, and the organizations pressing this common agenda had overlapping leadership and coordinated programs. One might leave the Kühl book with the impression that the story he relates has little to do with today, except for some fringe racists and some generalized cautions about the moral obtuseness of scientific expertise. In fact, today's disputes over abortion, euthanasia, fetal experimentation, and population control are on a continuum with the scientific culture of death examined by Stefan Kühl. He does, almost in passing, note the extraordinary role of the Rockefeller Foundation in pushing the eugenics agenda from the start. Rockefeller funded numerous conferences and research projects that were a great boost to Nazi-American collaboration, and the role of the foundation was generously appreciated by the Germans for giving their efforts international respectability.

Today Rockefeller is joined by Ford, MacArthur, and other megaphilanthropies that, together with a number of Western governments, pour hundreds of millions of dollars per year into promoting sterilization, abortion, and other measures aimed at limiting the fecundity of the poor and disadvantaged. All of this is done under the rubric of "population control," but it is in fact a massive exercise in negative eugenics. The racial, cultural, and economic presuppositions undergirding it are usually thinly disguised, and sometimes openly admitted. As Nicholas Eberstadt's thorough examination demonstrates (FIRST THINGS, January 1994), population control is ideology disguised as science. There is no scientific measure of "overpopulation," but there is a powerful and ideologically driven dread of lesser breeds that threaten our advantaged way of life and, presumably, the planetary balance.

We Americans are given to smugly assuring ourselves that "It can't happen here." And of course the full horror of something like the Third Reich has not happened here and, God willing, will not. What has happened here, as Stefan Kühl so trenchantly demonstrates, is that many of the "brightest and best" of the American scientific and public policy community warmly endorsed the ideas, and some of the practices, that gave the world the Holocaust. After 1945 they drew back in repugnance from the consequences of their ideas but, with slight semantic changes, they continued and they continue to advance the same ideas. One of the prosecutors at Nuremberg explained how people could act so savagely: "There is only one step to take. You may not think it possible to take it; but I assure you that men I thought decent men did take it. You have only to decide that one group of human beings have lost their human rights." As a polity, the United States has long since taken that step with respect to unborn children. The proponents of euthanasia urge upon us further steps in deciding that those who cannot effectively assert their rights have no rights. At Nuremberg the prosecution argued that the killing programs unfolded quite predictably from one thing to another, that the killing of the six-millionth Jew was set in motion by the morphine overdose given the first harelipped child.

Most of us rebel against the drawing of any analogies between ourselves and the Nazis. That is understandable. The rebellion is rooted in part in our conceit that we are not capable of such great evil. It is rooted also in an entirely reasonable appreciation of the differences between our circumstance—culturally, politically, economically—and that of Germany in the 1930s. But our perception of reality is distorted by making Nazism the test of evil. It is as though we can comfort ourselves that "it" is not happening here because there is no American Auschwitz and nobody is proposing the extermination of millions of Jews, gypsies, and others officially classified as subhuman.

So we allow, and even provide government subsidy for, the killing of 1.6 million unborn children each year. That, we are told, is no analogy with the Nazis because they prohibited abortion, at least for the socially desirable. So, moreover, it is open season for fetal experimentation, fetal farming, and the use of aborted corpses for transplants. That, we are told, is not comparable to doing the same thing with born children and grown-ups—and of course it both is and is not the same thing. It is not the same thing chiefly because we have decided that a group of human beings have no rights. So, yet further, the incidence of involuntary euthanasia (killing people who do not want to be killed) may one day reach the level that it is today in the Netherlands. That would be many thousands of killings per year. Even then, we will be told, that is nowhere near the scale of the Holocaust and, anyway, many of those people might want to be killed if they only knew what was best for them.

By making the Holocaust the measure of evil, we set an unreasonably high standard, so to speak. Whatever we have done and now do and may do in the future, it is certainly not that bad. It is as though we were to take a somewhat relaxed view of murderers who operate on a scale that falls short of Charles Manson or Jeffrey Dahmer. But then we remember the rabbinic wisdom that to save one life is to save the world; and its obverse, to kill one life is to kill the world. Not literally, of course, but morally, which is much more important. Genocide began with the first morphine overdose given a harelipped baby. Stefan Kühl's *The Nazi Connection* documents much more than its author knows, or at least much more than he says. It makes disturbingly clear that many of the most respectable, most influential, and most progressive scientific minds of this century laid the intellectual and moral ground- work on which the Nazis built, and cheered them on as they were building.

Later, most of these Nazi sympathizers would adamantly insist that that is not what they had meant, that is not what they meant at all. But the ideas are what matter, and in many cases they did not and have not disowned the ideas. The word "eugenics" does not appear in the annual report of the Rockefeller Foundation, but it does not take a cryptologist to recognize the euphemisms. "It" assumes many forms. While we work ourselves up into a fine heat shouting "Never again!" it is happening again. (*August/September 1994*)

FT

WHILE WE'RE AT IT

■ We received this some months ago and are not sure whether the publication in question survived or not. It's a nice color brochure that invites us to "Test Drive *New Theology Review* Absolutely Free!" The liberationist Presbyterian Robert McAfee Brown likes it. He says, "Although it has a clear Catholic orientation, members of other religious traditions will profit from its pages." The "although" is a nice touch, we thought. The brochure says that readers "will find the most current treatment of issues at the heart of their lives and voca- tions." The review "covers the broad plane of theology, seek- ing the most recent interpretations and insights." In sum,

"New Theology Review is your key to the latest and best in Christian theology!" Being very doubtful that the latest is best, we are inclined to take our theology old, so did not subscribe. We did notice that the magazine is published by The Liturgical Press at St. John's Abbey in Collegeville, Minnesota, and that was occasion for remembering how, oh so very many years ago, St. John's Abbey was a vibrant center of theological and pastoral renewal. You pay a price for not subscribing, of course. Now we're going to miss what the brochure announces as major themes coming up in the magazine: satanism, theology and ecology, and the challenge to Christian ethics posed by biomedical practices. Shouldn't that be the challenge to biomedical practices posed by Christian ethics? Ah well, there you have it; that old theology raising silly questions again. (*April 1994*)

■ So you think it's easy to be politically correct. Incorrect. A professor friend writes that he gave a lecture at a university and, the way you are supposed to these days, he inserted an occasional "she" into the text. Talking about a believer and an atheist, he made the atheist "she." The first "question" following the lecture strongly challenged his using the feminine for the atheist. The next time he gave the lecture, at another university, the believer was "she" and the atheist "he." Sure enough, the first "question" protested his stereotyping men as hardboiled and rational while females are soft and emotional. "What's a PC professor to do?" he asks. Another professor friend says he takes a different tack. At the start of his course he declares that his feminist convictions prevent him from going along with the idea that centuries of English literature using "he" were not influenced by women. Therefore, he defiantly asserts, he will use "he" to include both men and women, thus appropriating the tradition for the feminist cause. He reports that the students general approve of his "radical" linguistic tactic. The doleful conclusion is that many of today's college students are as dim-witted as their (plural of her/his) PC teachers. (*April 1994*)

■   From the "Weddings" page of the *Atlanta Journal-*

Constitution, a report on the marriage of Mark and Michelle Sadiq Manson: "Since Mark is Catholic and Michelle is Muslim, the two were married in a Methodist ceremony." Splitting the difference, so to speak. *(March 1994)*

■ Those crazy right-wingers are prone to the most bizarre hyperbole. Consider this evaluation of the influence of the far left ("the party of change") in American Catholicism: "The party of change seems to embrace just about every active minister in the Church, with the exception of a large number of bishops and some conservative younger clergy. It dominates the fields of liturgy, religious education, justice and peace offices, campus ministry, Catholic higher education, much popular spirituality, and the discipline of theology as a whole." The speaker is not some fevered traditionalist but Father Richard McBrien, former Chairman of Theology at Notre Dame, in a keynote address to a "Future of the Church" conference in Washington, D.C. He also called for stripping the papacy of its powers by "decentralizing" the Church. In his vision, local churches would elect their own bishops and "send a letter to Rome just to let them know, as a courtesy before they announce it." McBrien acknowledged that some people "find it very difficult to see how someone like me and others who criticize the authority of the Church are at the same time absolutely loyal to the Church." Among the enemies of change, whom he compared to the Stalinist coup leaders who tried to oust Gorbachev, McBrien puts at the top of the list Pope John Paul II and his doctrinal aide Joseph Cardinal Ratzinger. At a press conference he hinted that Ratzinger might have a Nazi past. "Keep in mind," he said, "Cardinal Ratzinger was a teenager during the Third Reich. We don't know what he was doing. Was he in the Hitler Youth? Some suggest he was." This may not be a new low in leftist smear tactics, but it is surely a candidate for that distinction. *(January 1992)*

■ "Do you believe Jesus is God?" "No," says Bishop John Spong (Episcopalian) of Newark, but "I do believe something of him was perfectly transparent to God." (He did not specify which part of Jesus might be transparent.) The statement prompted a reader of the *Christian Challenge*, which styles itself "The Only Worldwide Voice of Traditional Anglicanism," to come up with some revised titles for favorite hymns: "Clearer My God Through Thee," "Glass of Ages, Cleaned for Me," and "Joyful Joyful, We See Through Thee." Oh, those Anglicans. (*December 1994*)

LIKE FATHER LIKE SON, ALMOST

On a more personal note, but one not unrelated to the concerns addressed in these pages, my sister Mildred has been sorting through the heaps of letters, photos, and family oddments accumulated by Mom before she moved to the nursing home a few months ago at age ninety-two. Mildred has been mailing packets of selected materials to the eight children, and I am surprised to be learning things about my parents different from what I thought I knew. As with most small children, I suppose, I was endlessly fascinated by my parents' stories about "the olden days," meaning mainly the mid-1920s to the mid-1930s, the decade before my birth. Years ago I wrote out a reflection by a Llewelyn Powys and recently came across it again: "The years lived by our father before he begot us have upon them a wonder that cannot easily be matched. . . . In some dim way we share in those adventures of this mortal who not so long ago moved over the face of the earth like a god to call us up out of the deep."

The packet reveals that I wrote more often to my folks than I had remembered, in more detail, and more affectionately. Dad died at age seventy-two in 1972, and I have often thought that the life I have lived is in very large part his, but that is a long and complicated story that need not delay us here. More to the point is a document in the packet sent by Mim that is dated May 14, 1941. It is a paper given by the Rev. C. H. Neuhaus to the Ontario District Pastoral Conference, and in it he challenges a proposal by the

Canadian government for the moral and religious education of
children in the public schools. Apparently the paper met with
the approval of his colleagues in the ministerium of the
Lutheran Church—Missouri Synod and was given some wider
distribution in Canadian church circles. It is, so far as I know,
the only extensive statement by Dad on religion and public
policy, and this son cannot read it without entertaining a
question about how it is that arguments and dispositions are
transmitted from one generation to another. I very much
doubt that it is in the genes. Certainly Dad and I had not discussed these matters in any detail, in fact hardly at all, and yet
I discover more than fifty years later that—with a smidgen of
difference here and there—his arguments are mine, and that
the issues he addressed in 1941 are not all that different from
those being disputed in 1994.

It was wartime of course, Canada having gone into it with
Britain in 1939, and the government, as is the wont of governments, wanted religion to rally more fervently around the
flag. (That was when Canada still had a flag, before Prime
Minister Lester Pearson fobbed off on the long-suffering
Canadians a red maple leaf contrivance that has all the grav-
itas of a supermarket logo.) The government proposed putting
religion courses into the public schools, such courses to be
taught by the several clergymen of each school district. Keep
in mind that in Ontario public schools were and are distinct
from "separate" schools, the latter being Catholic schools supported by public funds. For all practical purposes, public
schools were Protestant schools—Protestant being defined as
non-Catholic. Dad thought the government proposal a very
bad idea, and in these nine now yellowed single-spaced pages
he sets out twelve reasons for his opposition. (He was a most
methodical man.) I will but touch on some highlights.

First, he contended that the climate of wartime was not
conducive to "sober and calm deliberation" of such an important question. If the proposal must be considered, it should be
put off until after the war. Meanwhile, those clergy who
favored the proposal should not exploit their positions of
influence. As becomes evident, he had chiefly in mind the

clergy of the Anglican Church and the United Church of Canada, the mainline Protestant denominations toward which he harbored some suspicion. "Clergymen," he wrote, "are not 'a superior form of humanity.' 'Good intentions' on their part are no more worthy of special consideration in a *Democracy* than are the 'good intentions' of an atheist. The moment you depart from this ideal of *Democracy* you cease being democratic and are preparing the soil for future bureaucracy and dictatorship." It is noteworthy that throughout the paper "democracy" is upper case and underlined, which turns out to be no mere stylistic eccentricity.

Religious instruction in the public schools, Dad argued, "is one step toward State Religion." His animus toward state religion was grounded in the experience of the Saxons who fled the state church of Prussia and founded the Missouri Synod in 1847. It was also based in his pastoral experience with immigrants from state churches who produced their church tax receipts as bona fides of their good standing as Lutheran Christians. The religious instruction proposal was indeed a small step, but Dad urged that it be seen in the light of the ambitions of some to establish a national church. He made clear that he was not speaking of the Roman Catholic Church, for which he had considerable respect. "I mean two large Protestant denominations in Canada. Members and clergy of the one have made the impression on me that they believe their church should be The Official Church by right of inheritance or by virtue of the former special recognition by the British Crown. The other large body is on record with these words, 'that this settlement of unity may in due time, as far as Canada is concerned, take shape in a Church which may fittingly be described as national.'" The first denomination was, of course, the Anglican, and the second the United Church of Canada, which was formed by a merger of Presbyterians, Methodists, and some others in the 1920s. In a *Democracy*, Dad said, they can preach their ideas from their denominational housetops, but they should not be given access to "the housetop of tax-supported public schools."

Moreover, clergy cannot teach, as was proposed by the

government—a nondenominational religion. Dad wondered about the integrity of clergy who would go along with such a plan: "Will he not feel that he is a traitor to his own beliefs and to the church to which he has bound himself whenever he answers questions in such a manner as to give equal value to opposite views and interpretations?" Then, sounding for all the world like a premature postmodernist attacking putatively universal perspectives, Dad wrote, "My conviction is that, strictly speaking, there is no such thing as nondenominational religion. If you disagree in some point with all the existing denominations then you form a new denomination of at least one member, whether you give your denomination a name or not. To be without opinion or belief is simply not human." He had on occasion tried, he said, to present evenhandedly conflicting interpretations of matters of importance, and it was his consistent experience that, despite his efforts, his own convictions asserted themselves "most unexpectedly." He did not have much confidence that most clergy would even try to make the effort.

He also opposed the government scheme because it would be "a further hindrance to an eventual Democratic settlement of the problem now existing between public and separate schools." His "dream" was that one day all school taxes would go into a common fund from which either all churches or no church could get support for their own schools. "At present the state's money is being used to teach only one religion in one church's schools." He was not opposed to the Catholic separate schools; he simply wanted other churches to have the same opportunity. The scheme for teaching in the public schools a religion "designed to suit Christian, Jew, and atheist" would delay a more just arrangement by creating a delusion among the majority Protestants that the question of religious instruction had been satisfactorily resolved, when in fact the religion being taught would satisfy almost nobody's idea of authentic religion.

Such instruction would, however, be identifiably Christian in some watered-down sense of the term, and that poses problems for non-Christians, no matter how small a minority they might be. The government scheme allowed that non-Christian children could be excused from religious instruction, but Dad thought that not nearly enough. He imagined a Jewish child thinking this way: "My father is a law-abiding citizen of this country which calls itself a *Democracy*. He is supposed to have the same rights and privileges as any other citizen of the land. When he pays his taxes the government never gives him a rebate because I do not get our kind of religion in the public schools. They say to my father that the religious instruction must be taken from the Christian Bible. If my father complains that this is not fair, he is told, 'If you don't like our arrangement, your boy can stay out during that time.' Queer thing this *Democracy*. You belong to it part of the time and part of the time you don't really belong." Dad opines, "Even a small neighborhood gang of boys demonstrates the true spirit of *Democracy* better than that. Will such a gang invoke the majority rule and insist on cooking a rabbit stew on Friday when they know that only one member, Mickey O'Brien, is not to eat meat on Friday?"

Moreover, an hour or two a week of such religious instruction would not be able to compete with the "pseudo-science" of secularism that is otherwise taught in the schools. "Which theory is going to be upheld, that monkeys became evolutionists or that evolutionists became monkeys?" Then too, sound moral instruction is unlikely since the clergy do not agree on the nature of sin or even on what is a sin. Among the examples he cites: "Will one condemn the modern mixed dance as sin and another classify it as highly desirable rhythmic recreation? Will one try to make the children believe that the Sabbath-laws of the Old Testament are still in force while another will say that they were abolished when Christ came? Will one present moderate drinking as a crime and another insist that only drunkenness is sin?" (The Missouri Synod was against dancing, indifferent to Sabbath laws, and positively disposed toward moderate drinking, with moderation very generously defined.)

Dad also opposed the government scheme because he thought many clergy did not "stand for true principles of patriotism." He had the "rabid pacifists" of the liberal church-es in mind, but he also worried about those who "taught a shallow, supercilious, hysterical brand of patriotism [that swings] too far towards the opposite extreme." He observed, "Just being a member of the clergy was no guarantee for a man's patriotism in the last war [World War I] and certainly is not so today." One detects a little needling of the establish-mentarian mainline going on here. In World War I, German Lutherans were suspected of having a "dual loyalty," if they were not actually traitors. There were some instances of vio-lence against Lutheran pastors, and almost everywhere there was pressure to drop German language services and other evi-dences of "foreignness." In 1941, by contrast, this German Lutheran pastor presents himself as the guardian of "true patri-otism" against the mainline pacifists, on the one hand, and jingoists, on the other. Dad knew a thing or two about posi-tioning oneself to forensic advantage.

In his most detailed objection to the government propos-al, he excoriates the churches for evading their responsibility for the religious education of their children. Religious instruc-tion in the public schools is a deceptively easy way out. "How disgracefully cheap is this arrangement! Cheapness in reli-gious instruction has for so long been in vogue among the churches that the temptation to get still more even cheaper instruction by putting religion into the public schools is all but irresistible to some." Then, in his twelfth objection, he returns to the question of fairness. "There is a minority in our *Democracy* which prefers not to be bothered with our religion. For us to try to force religion on them in a public tax-support-ed school because we claim it is good for them may have the best intentions behind it, but nevertheless it is dangerous rea-soning in a *Democracy*. . . . In a *Democracy* we love to speak of our sportsmanship. If you heard a person talking about shoot-ing a fine buck and knew all the while that he had first set a snare for that buck to make sure that it couldn't get away, you'd be thoroughly disgusted with that man." The school tru-ancy laws, he suggested, were like that snare; giving clergy a captive audience for their instruction. "I do not believe," he said in summary, "that this is becoming to a *Democracy*." (The analogy of children as targets should perhaps not be pressed too far, but Dad was an almost obsessive hunter and the analogy no doubt seemed to him quite natural.)

I suggested earlier that, mutatis mutandis, Dad's attitudes and arguments then were pretty close to mine now. The suspicion of civil religion or any religion under government auspices, the need for undiluted Christian witness, the imperative to respect differences, the devotion to democratic fairness, the impossibility of neutrality in matters of religious and moral consequence—all these seem as pertinent today as they were in the disputes of 1941. His "dream" of a common public fund from which people could get support for the schools of their choice is today's advocacy of vouchers and other measures to give parents real decision-making power in education. I suppose some readers might even detect a connection between Dad's objection to the pretensions of mainline churches and this writer's occasional criticisms of old-line liberalism in this country. If there is such a connection, it is not in the genes; it is in the continuing confusions of liberal Protestantism. Dad, who was by his seminary classmates called "Pope" Neuhaus, was a man of rather definite views. That, of course, is another difference between father and son.

As it happened, the scheme that Dad was protesting did go through, although he refused to participate in it. In my grade school we had Canon Phillips, the Anglican rector, come in once a week for our spiritual edification. Out of hearing, we students referred to him as "Canonball Phillips" and thought him awfully dull. I remember thinking him not too sharp as well, since he always got the numbering of the Ten Commandments wrong (Lutherans and Catholics count them the right way). He was a soft-spoken and no doubt quite admirable person, but Canon Phillips made no discernible impact on my spiritual consciousness, and certainly posed no serious religious alternative to a boy steeped in the true faith as promulgated by the Missouri Synod. The Catholics were something else; they were seriously different. In religious education, and perhaps in other respects, Dad wanted what the

Catholics had. I expect he and Father Harrington of St. John the Baptist talked about such matters on their long deer hunting expeditions up in Algonquin country. They almost always came back with a fine buck or doe, usually with two. And I am sure they set no snares. (*August/September 1994*)

FT

THE PRODIGAL NUN

A difficulty is that there are so many versions of the Bible around nowadays that one doesn't know what is supposed to be a translation, a paraphrase, a revisionist redaction, or the discovery of some new manuscript. A biblical scholar of our acquaintance suggests that what follows, "The Parable of the Prodigal Nun," may belong to the last category. "There was a bishop who had two daughters; and the elder of them said, Father, give me the portion of thy substance that falleth to me. And he divided unto them his living. And not many days after the elder gathered all together, and took her journey unto the Summer Pastoral Institute of Notre Dame University, and there wasted her substance with riotous living and liturgies. And when she had spent all, there arose a radical tide in that land, and she began to feel left out. And she went and joined herself to one of the lesbians of that country, and she sent her into the missile bases to bait swine. And she would fain have graced her Volvo with one of the bumper stickers at which the swine did scoff, but no one gave unto her. But when she came to herself she said, How many of my father's hirelings have desktop publishing capability and to spare, and I languish here with mimeos. I will arise and go to my father and will say unto him, Father, thou hast sinned against heaven and in my sight; thou art no longer worthy to be called my sire; treat me as one of thy committee chairpersons. And she arose and came to her father. But when she was yet afar off, the bishop saw her, and was moved with guilt, and ran, and tripped on his sandal, and kissed her feet. And the daughter said unto him, Father thou hast harassed me by salivating on my toenails during office hours; but do thou make me as supreme coordinator of thy chancery. And the father said to his secretaries, Bring forth quickly the Mac Plus with the laser printer and place it in her office, and put a cellular phone in the Buick, and bring the fatted cleric and sack him, and let us make caring, for this my daughter was bored and found life, and we were out of it, and yea are deemed with it again. And they began to share. Now his younger daughter was in the chapel, and as she came and drew nigh to the Activities Center, she heard music and dancing. And she paged one of the secretaries, and inquired what these things might be, and she said unto her, Thy sister is come, and the bishop hath sacked Monsignor Riordan, because thy sire she hath accepted as a partner in ministry. But she was in sore despond, and had baby clothes to pack for the Birthright drive, and did not come in. And her father came out and scolded her. But she answered and said to the bishop, Lo these many years do I serve thee, and I never transgressed a memorandum of thine, and yet thou never gavest me a magic marker, that I might make flyers with my friends. But when this daughter came, which hath devoured thy living with the People's Committee for Reproductive Freedom in Nicaragua, thou cannest for her the seminary rector. And he said unto her, Look, sweetheart, thou art not going nowhere, even if I locked up the Ko-Rec-Type on thee, which I've got half a mind to do. But it is meet to make sharing and be glad, for CBS News is due here in fifteen minutes with a film crew. Get thee hence then into the media blackout, where there is non-inclusive wailing and gnashing of teeth. And he issued a directive that the door be bolted behind her." *(May 1994)*

FT

RELIGION AND
WHAT PASSES FOR THE NEWS

People want a lot more news about religion than they're getting. At least that is the finding of a major national study conducted by Religious News Service (RNS) and funded by the Lilly Endowment. Note that in the interviews people were not alerted to the fact that the study had any religious connection. They were simply asked what kinds of news most interested them. Religion was way up there. Way ahead of gossip, the culture page, astrology, business, and sports. "Way ahead of sports?!" a colleague asked, incredulous. This colleague, be it known, is a sports freak with a special devotion to the Orioles, which we understand to be a baseball team in Baltimore. Devout Catholic though he is, we have no doubt that he would turn to the baseball standings before reading the story on the election of a new pope.

"If people said that they're more interested in religion than sports," he declared, "they're lying." But why should people lie about that? Surely in our culture of privatized religion it is more respectable to tell a stranger that you're very interested in sports than that you're very interested in religion. The overall results of this study are no doubt affected also by a gender difference, most women being less obsessed by sports than is our friend. (Most men, too, for that matter.) But back to the main point. Despite the high level of interest in religion news, consider the difference in coverage of religion and sports in both print and broadcast media. Fifty-to-one in favor of sports would be a very conservative estimate. If creatures from another planet were to get their information about life in America from the news media, it would come to them as a stunning surprise that more Americans attend church or synagogue *every week* than attend all professional sports events in an entire year

There are a number of reasons the media ignore the largest single pattern of voluntary associational behavior in our society. Studies by Rothman and Lichter have demonstrated the dramatic gap in religious belief and behavior between news executives and the general population. In addition, religion news is thought to be so upbeat as to be soporific. Good news is no news. Scandals—especially if they involve Fundamentalists or Catholics—get considerable coverage, as do theological battles leading to denominational breakups. Almost any public fight with the Pope is thought to be news-worthy. But that's about it.

Complaints that religion does not receive enough news attention may he dismissed as self-serving. The Lilly-RNS study suggests, however, that readers and viewers earnestly do want more coverage of religion, and one would think that might make an impression on news executives who cannot be entirely indifferent to market dynamics. Religion gets along just fine without the coverage. There are no doubt many reli-gious groups and leaders who prefer it that way. But if journal-ism is to make any pretense of representing the society—what matters to people and the institutions they care about—the ludicrously slight attention paid religion must be remedied. Did we mention that more than twice as many people are in church or synagogue every week than vote in presidential elec-tions once every four years? (*April 1991*)

FT

TWO NATIONS, SEPARATE AND UNEQUAL

"The Myth of Racial Progress" is an unfortunate title for a *Christianity Today* symposium among prominent black Evangelicals. By many important indices there has been enor-mous racial progress in the last quarter century. It would be tedious to point out all the ways in which blacks have advanced in recent years. At least economically, the majority of blacks are doing as well or better than whites of comparable age and educational achievement. The problem is not that there has not been progress; it is that the progress has not included everybody and that, ironically, progress for some has worsened the condition of others. The last is a point made by William Julius Wilson, the liberal black sociologist at the University of Chicago. The "radical isolation" of the black underclass in the inner cities, says Wilson, is in large part caused by the outlawing of racial discrimination that enabled middle-class blacks to move away from the inner cities, leaving the poorest blacks on their own.

William Pannell of Fuller Theological Seminary is part of the *Christianity Today* symposium. He has recently published *The Coming Race Wars?* (Zondervan). Although the question mark is a hedging of bets, Pannell's message is grim. In the symposium he says, "We're going to have to take some rather courageous and extraordinary steps to avoid a race war. The first step is sincere repentance of racism by white evangelicals. Until something like that happens, I don't envision black evangelicals taking their white counterparts seriously." One does not quite know what to make of that. Using such combustible language with great care, there is no denying that there is a lot that qualifies as racism among white Americans, evangelical and other. And a call to repentance is almost always in order, but white Americans of good will are increasingly confused about what they are supposed to repent of, and what help such repentance might be to blacks.

The Rev. Hycel Taylor of Second Baptist Church in Evanston, Illinois, takes a somewhat different tack. "For us, as an African-American people, we have to ask some serious questions. What's going wrong with us? Not so much in relationship to white people, but in relation to ourselves. What's so stigmatic in our minds that we have now turned on ourselves and begun to kill each other, where now we become our own lynch mobs? We're looking at genocide so insidious that if we quantified the dying of African Americans just for twenty-four hours across this nation, we'd need to call for a state of national emergency. We're dying of AIDS; we're dying of hypertension; we're dying as stillborn babies; we're dying from drugs."

These are the issues recently being pressed by the Rev.

Jesse Jackson, in a welcome return to some of the themes he championed before being taken captive to national politics. Jackson has been going around the country exhorting young blacks to take charge of their lives, pointing out that today in America there are more blacks killed by blacks every year than were lynched by whites in more than two hundred years of slavery. Similarly, the Rev. Earl Rivers of the Dorchester, Massachusetts, Azusa Christian Community has been attracting attention, both white and black, to the nature of the crisis. In the left-leaning *Boston Review* he has sparked a lively exchange around his argument that, within the fairly near future, more than half of young black men will be killed before they reach age twenty-five. Today, in addition to those who are dead, more than a quarter of black males under twenty-five are in the criminal justice system—imprisoned, awaiting trial or sentencing, or on parole.

There is no doubt that these doleful realities are related, more than to any other factor, to the dissolution of the black family. More than two-thirds of black children are born with no adult male accepting responsibility for them, and the figure reaches toward 90 percent in the inner cities. This pattern of male flight from the family, combined with misguided welfare policies that encourage girls to have babies and set up housekeeping on their own, have created an ominous set of problems that are tying public policy experts in knots. Lest white Americans be complacent, it is noted that nearly one-third of white children are now born without fathers who claim them. That is almost exactly the figure for black America thirty years ago, and in both cases the numbers are climbing. (Presumably, in the black inner city the increase will stop somewhere short of 100 percent.) All this constitutes crisis to be sure, crisis without parallel in American experience. But it is hard to know what it has to do with white repentance of racism.

Race wars seem highly improbable. For many years now, black militants have been doing their revolutionary shuffle, intimidating whites with the threat of racial violence. Whatever the merits of their cause, it simply isn't working anymore. This is part of the decline of a certain kind of liberalism; fewer whites have a cultivated appetite for feeling guilty about race. In addition, there is a confidence that the threatening population can be yet more radically isolated, by coercion if necessary. One fears that that is at least part of the popularity of "getting tough on crime" in our current politics. It is true, as the Kerner Commission said so many years ago, that we are "two nations, separate and unequal." It is more true today than it was then. Except the divide between the two nations is not racial. On the one side are whites, the majority of blacks, the great majority of Hispanics, and almost all Asians and other recent immigrants. On the other side of the divide is the urban underclass. For reasons that are at the heart of the formation and deformation of the American experiment, the distinction between black and white has a singular place in our moral consciousness. But it is increasingly less relevant to the political, cultural, and economic realities of American life.

President Clinton learned this when he played the race card in last year's mayoralty campaign in New York. At least one hopes he learned it. He suggested that people would not vote for David Dinkins because he is black. This did not sit well with most New Yorkers. For large numbers of white New Yorkers, the fact that Dinkins is black was the only good reason for voting for him. Weighing against it was his legendary incompetence and astonishing indifference to the sensibilities of those who are not black (or gay), notably Catholics and Jews. In New York, a very liberal city, just enough people had had enough of feeling guilty and being intimidated by threats of racial violence, and as a result Mr. Dinkins is now the former mayor.

The *Christianity Today* symposium resurrects the old line about eleven o'clock Sunday morning being the most segregated hour of the week. It was a good line, but surely it should be put back to sleep. Since the days of the civil rights movement, denominations that are almost totally white have devoutly adopted affirmative action programs for increasing black membership. Some old-line denominations embraced the idea that they wouldn't get over their racism until their black membership equaled the proportion of blacks in the general population, which is somewhat more than 10 percent. Of course to do this would require intensive evangelization among blacks, or outright sheep stealing from black churches. Needless to say, they did not consult the clergy of the black churches as to the advisability of this enterprise. Also needless to say, such recruitment programs did not get very far, and are not likely to go anywhere in the future. Nor should they. Whatever potential for moral and social renewal there is in the inner cities, it is very largely to be found in the black churches.

When it comes to concrete proposals, the symposiasts urge new linkages between black and white churches in urban and suburban areas. Perhaps some kind of "sister church" arrangement in which congregations simply visit each other from time to time. As an example, *Christianity Today* highlights a wealthy suburban congregation near Atlanta whose members went into the inner city to help blacks rebuild some dilapidated housing. Some will think such steps are awfully tame, and awfully old, and maybe just a little condescending on the part of whites. Perhaps they are all of that. Such steps do not have the frisson of revolutionary violence and radical change. But they bring the radically isolated (on both sides) into contact, and create the potential for building trust and friendship. Given the awful history of black-white relations in America, every such relationship of trust and friendship is to be valued as a good in itself.

Whites should be challenged to do what they can, but should not feel guilty about not doing what they cannot. No matter how repentant, compassionate, and eager they are, they cannot redress the moral and cultural deficit of the urban underclass. That must be done by black leaders who have the wisdom and courage to act on the new reality of race in America. This is not a case of letting whites off the hook. To suggest that is white arrogance and an insult to blacks. It assumes that the problem of the underclass must be resolved by whites. Why should blacks alone, of all the identifiable groups in America, be thought incompetent to take charge of their

lives? Slavery and enforced segregation were singular injus-
tices visited upon blacks. Both are now a long time ago. Even
under segregation, most blacks managed to take moral charge
of their lives. Since segregation, that continues to be the case,
but approximately a third at the bottom have become wards of
the welfare state living in circumstances of soul-destroying
dependency and lethal anarchy.

To the extent that whites are complicit in well-intended
but misguided social policies, this is a white problem. To the
extent that whites can help transcend the divide between
themselves and the radically isolated, this is a white obligation. But the reality of the urban underclass is overwhelmingly a black problem and a black obligation. And a black moral
opportunity. The sooner this is recognized by both blacks and
whites, the sooner we will move on from distracting talk about
"the myth of racial progress" to building the story of American
progress that includes everybody. (April 1994)

FT

THE RULING "WE"
OF THE AMERICAN JEWISH CONGRESS

Some writers on the First Amendment, including this editor,
have long made the argument that there is but one religion
clause. The purpose of the clause is to protect the "free exercise" of religion, and the "no establishment" provision is in
the service of that purpose (see "A New Order of Religious
Freedom," FIRST THINGS, February 1992). This approach is in
sharp contrast to those who would pit the "two clauses"
against one another. For example, Burt Neuborne, Professor of
Law at New York University. Writing in Congress Monthly, the
magazine of the American Jewish Congress, Neuborne exem-
plifies an extreme but very influential reading of the First
Amendment on religion.

Neuborne notes that free exercise requires us to defend religious behavior even when we strongly disagree with it. "Witness the fact that we will correctly defend someone's religious right not to be vaccinated against a contagious disease." At the same time, Neuborne writes, "the Establishment clause requires us to be suspicious of religion, even hostile to it. . . . One clause says that religion is something to be cherished, while the other says that religion is something to be feared." Neuborne approvingly describes this as the genius of "a schizophrenic Constitution—one that pulls us in different directions, one that pulls in favor of religion in its Free Exercise clause and against religion in its Establishment clause."

The reason "no establishment" is intended to inculcate fear and hostility toward religion, says Neuborne, is that religion, unlike politics, is not volitional. In addition, "What is both sublime and terrifying about religion is that it is essentially non-rational behavior. . . . You don't carry on a reasoned dialogue about your relationship with your God. Religion is there and you live it." And so it was that "the Founders inserted the Free Exercise clause, designed to shelter individuals who were driven to act by a force more powerful than law." Free exercise, according to Neuborne, "requires us to carve out a special niche of toleration" for such nonrational behavior. Religion is not only nonrational, but too many of its proponents are irrational. "Try," Neuborne writes, "having a reasoned discussion with Pat Buchanan or Pat Robertson."

A "prophylactic wall between church and state" is required to protect the public square from religion. Neuborne concludes: "We have not been ashamed to say that we cherish religion and will protect its private exercise to the very limit of reason—and perhaps a little beyond. Conversely, we have not been afraid to acknowledge that we fear public religion and that we are committed to preventing it from getting a toehold in the country's government."

Although others do not put it in such flat-footed language—they would not, for instance, come right out and say that "no establishment" requires hostility to religion—the views of Professor Neuborne are widely shared. They underlie and are sometimes explicitly stated in numerous court decisions. The problem with the Neuborne interpretation is that it flies in the face of the plain reading of the religion clause of the First Amendment. And it flies in the face of what we know to be the intention of the Founders (see, for example, William Lee Miller, *The First Liberty*, or John Noonan, *The Believer and the Powers That Are*). Neuborne's is truly a new born interpretation that has a provenance of no more than fifty years, its godfather being the formidable and self-described extreme separationist, Leo Pfeffer of the American Jewish Congress.

This extreme interpretation is certainly not held by all Jews nor by all Jewish organizations. In fact, one of the very encouraging developments of recent years is the growing skepticism of thoughtful Jews toward "strict separationism." (The Ethics and Public Policy Center in Washington, D.C. has just published a book-length collection of "revisionist" Jewish reflections on religion and public life: *American Jews and the Separationist Faith*, edited by David G. Dalin.) Nonetheless, the Pfefferian reading of the First Amendment, as represented by Neuborne and the Congress, is still the dominant view among American Jews, and in many of our courts.

Neuborne's contorted interpretation of the First Amendment is matched by his curious view that religion is nonrational. Admittedly, Neuborne's view is hardly novel, but it is sharply contested by innumerable Christians and Jews who understand the religious life indeed to be the carrying on of a "reasoned dialogue" with God—although they might not choose that precise language. Ironically, Neuborne's claim is that the Constitution "establishes" a brand of religion—espoused in both existentialist and traditionalist versions—that asserts that faith is a matter of blind and unreasoned submission to authority. That is not the religion of most Christians and most Jews. Further, Neuborne would "establish" a religion that is entirely individual and private, that is hermetically sealed off from the public sphere. That is certainly not the religion of Christians, Jews, and Muslims whose faith is emphatically communal and public in character

The Pfefferian inversion of the religion clause that continues to be promoted by the American Jewish Congress subordi-
nates "free exercise" (the end) to "no establishment" (a means
to that end). It does so by establishing a religion that is in conflict with the religion espoused by the great majority of
Americans, and by propounding a profoundly anti-democratic
interpretation of our constitutional order. The Constitution
requires, says Neuborne, "that we fear public religion and that
we are committed to preventing it from getting a toehold in the
country's government." This is inescapably an argument against
democratic governance. If, as we know to be the case, most
Americans claim to derive their moral discernments from religion—however confusedly they may do so—to exclude religion
from the ordering of our public life is to exclude the discernments, judgments, and aspirations of the sovereign people from
whom democracy derives its moral legitimacy.

Then there is the offputting snobbery in Neuborne's argument. "Try having a reasoned discussion with Pat Buchanan or
Pat Robertson," he says. To which one might counter, "Try
having a reasoned discussion with Burt Neuborne about, for
instance, the nature of religion and public life." (The present
writer is pleased to report that, in fact, he has had reasoned
discussions with all three of the gentlemen in question.) Of
those whom he calls "the religiously driven" Neuborne writes,
"As individuals, we cherish and tolerate them; as political
actors, we fear and control them." Really now. Who belongs to
this "we" that presumes to "control" millions of Americans
who, by Neuborne's definition, are "religiously driven"?
Thoughtful Americans of all political and religious persuasions
are fully justified in dismissing with scorn, and not a little
resentment, the legally contorted and brazenly elitist pre-
sumption of Professor Neuborne and the American Jewish
Congress. (*February 1993*)

ANTICIPATORY SURRENDER

It is offensively religious, said a state of California social service bureaucrat a few years ago, for a center serving the poor to be called the Saint Vincent De Paul Center. And, in view of the center's involvement in government programs, retaining the name is probably also unconstitutional, it was suggested. The problem was not so much with the name as with the "Saint." Now if we could refer to him as Mr. Vincent De Paul there would be no difficulty. Silly? Of course, but not unrepresentative of government officials obsessed with a distorted notion of the separation of church and state; and, regrettably, not unrepresentative of church officials eager not to get on the wrong side of the state.

Here is an item from the *Saint Paul Pioneer Press* in Minnesota. (One notes there is no serious movement underway to change the name of the city.) US West Direct has excised religious symbols and references from its new edition of the yellow pages. Two religiously based adult care programs, St. Benedict's Center and Good Shepherd Lutheran Home, have been told that their ads are "discriminatory." St. Benedict's had to remove its logo, which includes a cross, and could use "Benedict" in its ad only once because of its religious connotations. Good Shepherd could not use its shepherd staff logo and could print "Good Shepherd" only once. In forbidding religion-specific advertising, US West Direct invokes the federal Fair Housing Act, which prohibits religious discrimination.

The two homes claim that the policy violates their religious freedom and that of their clients. Suzanne Hartley of Good Shepherd says that, if the home does not designate itself as religion-based, it could lose clients seeking that particular environment and attract others who don't want it. Ms. Hartley is undoubtedly on the side of the angels on this one, but one wonders if she understands the larger issue. The larger issue is that the dynamics of government mandated nondiscrimination require that places such as St. Benedict's and Good Shepherd should not be religiously distinctive. To be distinctive is to run the risk of attracting people who favor the distinction in question and thereby to become complicit in "discrimination." Thus do terms such as "nondiscrimination," "pluralistic," and "inclusive" get transmogrified into government-enforced uniformity and homogeneity.

The Fair Housing Act is not supposed to apply to religious institutions such as these nursing homes. And nobody accuses the homes of actually discriminating against anyone. Their crime is that they are different and, by being different, invite applications from old people who would like to be in a Catholic or Lutheran home. Such old folk, though guilty of discrimination, probably don't know any better; but the homes, by advertising what makes them different, have no excuse and become accomplices in the offense. To be fair, the government is not saying that these homes cannot be distinctively religious in the way they present themselves to the public. US West Direct is saying that. But it is saying it out of fear of what the government regulators might do, and it is imposing its fear upon the homes. This might be called anticipatory surrender. When in doubt about what the state requires, assume the worst and cave in. With such deeds of spinelessness large and small the road to serfdom is paved. The "yellow" in yellow pages takes on new meaning. *(May 1994)*

FT

DEMOCRATIC CONSERVATISM

A question much discussed in the last few years was what would happen to the "conservative coalition" after the Peace of Reagan. We did not have to wait long to find out. Infighting among conservatives has a venerable pedigree. Some who view the last eight years as an aberration appear delighted to resume the tradition. Others, believing that "the conservative revolution" has hardly begun, think there are more important things to do than indulge intramural squabbles.

In an earlier fight, the redoubtable Russell Kirk termed libertarians "the chirping sectaries" of the right. That may become the apt term for a little band of conservatives who declare themselves the keepers of the flame and seem to be declaring what could become a nasty little war against those whom they view as imposters. Democracy is their *bête noir*, and they vent their animus most specifically at "neoconservatives," who are variously derided as democratists, global democrats, political parasites, and ideological mercenaries. The tone of the attack is less than edifying.

Denominational tags are disputed, but the sectaries on the attack are usually called paleoconservatives—as distinct from the old right, the new right, the religious right, and, above all, the neoconservatives. "Paleos" are, in a nutshell, at war with modernity. Theirs tends to be a patrician view of republican governance conducted by men of tested genetic stock. In the way they tell it, the American story is one of almost unremitting decline. With Henry Adams a century ago and Gore Vidal today, they believe that modernity and her rapacious consorts, democracy and capitalism, have sold America into bondage to immigrant newcomers who, in their grasping vulgarity, know nothing of republican virtue. The paleos quietly seethed while Ronald Reagan championed a conservatism of democracy, capitalism, and progress, but now they're not going to take it anymore.

Beyond the paleo war against "democratism," one notes renewed attempts to invite back into the conservative movement a list of uglies that had long been consigned to the fever swamps, in large part by the efforts of William F. Buckley and his *National Review*. The list includes nativism, racism, anti-Semitism, xenophobia, a penchant for authoritarian politics, and related diseases of the *ressentiment* that flourishes on the marginalia of American life. There will always be some who enjoy the *frisson* of flirting with forbidden bigotries once confused with conservatism. No conservative should need to be told that terms such as racism and anti-Semitism can be abused to quash the discussion of legitimate issues, but some may need to be reminded that the evils signified by such terms are not merely figments of the fevered liberal imagination.

One can understand the desire of some conservatives to have "their" movement back again, to reclaim it from those whom they view as assertive newcomers. Fortunately, most conservatives do not believe that an expanding movement is a sign of apostasy, or that arguments can only be won at the price of integrity lost. They have been persuaded that effectiveness in the defense of truth is no vice, and impotence in the pursuit of justice is no virtue. While able to accept honorable defeat, they do not think defeat is a moral imperative. Not content to grouse, they are prepared to govern.

Spanning Generations

In contrast to the chirping sectaries of a factious past, a new generation of thinkers is coming on line. They know that our society is embroiled in a great *Kulturkampf*, and the war will be won or lost on the terrain of the ideas we take to be most bindingly true. The religio-cultural battle is not the only one, but it is the most critical battle. Defining the moral symbols and truth claims by which a people lives can redefine the democratic idea to which this people is inveterately attached.

Authentic religion cannot be the servant of American democracy, or of any political order short of the Kingdom of God. The essential paradox is that religion is most politically potent when it debunks the pretensions of the political, keeping the City of Man under the transcendent judgment of the City of God. Thus religion's contribution to the renewal of democracy depends, first, upon the renewal of religion. This way of thinking can provide a nuanced account of democratic governance that is limited, constitutional, and accountable to what some call natural law and the common good. Happily, there are projects advancing this way of thinking underway in the worlds of Judaism, Evangelicalism, and even old-line Protestantism. Those who view these efforts as selling out to the liberal god of "democratism" lost track of the discussion some while back.

And the discussion does go back some while. In the last year much ink has been spent on the paleo-neo wars, but the lineaments of the dispute have been evident for at least three decades. Consider, for example, Will Herberg's masterful 1956 essay on Reinhold Niebuhr as a representative of the "new conservatism." Herberg noted that Niebuhr was embarrassed about being perceived as a conservative, as indeed are some who are called neoconservative today. Then much more than now, however, the embarrassment was understandable, since thirty years ago "conservatism" generally referred to positions and dispositions now associated with the "paleos."

Yet Herberg correctly saw that "the basic direction of Niebuhr's political philosophy" required the term conservative. Niebuhr had by the 1940s arrived at a decisive critique of modern political thought as that thought was grounded in the French Enlightenment. In 1944 he described the French Enlightenment as the cradle of "every error which infects a modern liberal culture in its estimate of the human situation, and of most of the errors which reached a tragic culmination in modern totalitarianism." The French Revolution, he wrote, "produced despotism in the name of liberty, civil war in the name of fraternity, and superstitious politics in the name of reason." According to Herberg, what was "new" in Niebuhr's conservatism was that it did not repudiate the core of his earlier radicalism.

Herberg wrote that Niebuhr's "prophetic radicalism implied a radical relativization of all political programs, institutions, and movements, and therefore a thoroughgoing rejection of every form of political rationalism. Add to this a renewed emphasis on the historic continuities of social life, and Niebuhr's brand of 'conservatism' emerges. It is manifestly not the conservatism of those who are called conservatives in American public life today [i.e., 1956], but it is enough apparently to establish a kinship with Burke and to give Niebuhr a prominent place in all the recent histories and anthologies of the 'new conservatism.'"

The new conservatism of 1956 is the neoconservatism of 1990. Reinhold Niebuhr's nuanced appreciation of democracy had internalized and gone beyond the polemics against "democratism" that are still being echoed by some conservatives in 1990. As we said, these polemicists lost track of the discussion some while back. *(March 1990)*

FT

MORALISM'S DEADLY "CONSISTENCY"

The culture war is not between the moral and the immoral parties. Rather; there are moralities in bitter conflict. The one is a morality, typically shaped by biblical faith, based on moral truth, aspiration, and forgiveness. The other, typically irreligious or antireligious, assumes "moral truth" is an oxymoron and presses ideological claims with unforgiving rigidity. It is more aptly described as moralistic. This was brought to mind by a file of items from last fall. Readers may recall the media explosion when, in an interview, Dan Quayle said that he would still love his daughter even if she did the terribly wrong thing of having an abortion. Headlines declared that Quayle was "waffling" and "backtracking" on his pro-life commitment. What did the reporters expect Quayle to say? That he would disown his daughter; throw her out of the house, and never speak to her again? Yes, it was implied, that would be the appropriate reaction if he were "morally consistent." At about the same time, gay activists "outed" John Schlafly, son of Phyllis Schlafly. His mother declared, "I love my son," and the gay press, joined by what styles itself as the mainstream press, chortled over the exposure of Phyllis Schlafly's "hypocrisy." Presumably, if she were really sincere in her criticism of homosexuality, she would hate her son.

The culture war is in large part a conflict between morality and moralism. The former evidences a sense of humor, an awareness of the fragility of the human condition, a readiness to bear with one another in our imperfections, and the heart to aspire anew to the excellence of which we are capable. The moralism of the politically correct, on the other hand, is humorless, relentless, demanding, deadly. It is a glaring anomaly of our time that such moralism claims a monopoly on the term "compassion," a disposition that it cannot understand and so angrily scorns. The explanation, as the wise have been observing for centuries, is the failure to acknowledge the reality of original sin, the only Christian doctrine that is verifiable beyond the possibility of reasonable doubt. Moralistic consistency is, if we may paraphrase, the hobgoblin of little souls. The sadness is that such people cannot accept for themselves or others the forgiveness without which life is the living hell of moralistic correctness. The conformist wisdom in our elite culture is that religion is the source of moral oppression, and much religion can be faulted on that score. The alternative often proposed is liberation from moralism that turns out to be liberation from morality. Typically, those who leave religious moralism behind are most vulnerable to the fevers of ideological moralism. None of us has perfect immunity from the infections of moralism, religious or otherwise. The only moral consistency that is not lethal begins and ends in grace. As in, for example, "Forgive us our sins as we forgive those who sin against us." As in Quayle forgives his daughter; Schlafly forgives her son, and both, we expect, forgive those who accuse them of being morally inconsistent. (*March 1993*)

FT

WHILE WE'RE AT IT

■ Superior Court Justice Bernard Carter of Crown Point, Indiana, has come up with an interesting approach to sentencing. It seems fourteen students of Collegians Activated to Liberate Life (CALL) were convicted of trespassing at an abortuary. Carter sentenced them to spend eight hours in a class taught by Planned Parenthood. Arthur Delaney of Philadelphia, who brought this item to our attention, suggests that the Carter approach has almost infinite possibilities.

Those protesting prostitution in their streets could be sentenced to live in a brothel for a time, antipornography protesters could be made to watch skin flicks, and so forth. The purpose of justice, presumably, is to make the punishment fit the crime. The crime of which the fourteen students were convicted was trespassing. In Judge Bernard Carter's view, however, the crime is that the students hold the wrong position on abortion. Strange how people keep saying that it can't happen here. (*March 1994*)

■ To date he is unknown here, but in Finland he is a celebrity and there appears to be a growing number of Americans ready for his message. Pentti Linkola is a writer who supports himself by fishing in a rustic region, and lives in order to save the planet by means of annihilating most of the human race. He proposes ending third world aid and asylum for refugees, plus mandatory abortions for women who already have two children. Another world war would be "a happy occasion for the planet," he suggests. Humanity is like a sinking ship with 100 passengers and a lifeboat that can hold only ten. "Those who hate life try to pull more people on board and drown everybody. Those who love and respect life use axes to chop off the extra hands hanging on the gunwale." Mr. Linkola's sworn enemies, reasonably enough, are the Pope and Amnesty International. He also despises America. "The U.S. symbolizes the worst ideologies in the world: growth and freedom." In Finland, where he is described as an "eco-fascist," Linkola is an exceedingly popular author. A *Wall Street Journal* story notes that even fellow Malthusians in this country find Linkola a bit much. "We have many possibilities that should be explored before we take a strong-armed approach," says Garret Hardin, who in 1974 wrote a much discussed article, "Living on a Lifeboat." Dr. Hardin has never been accused of squeamishness when it comes to reducing the number of those whom he views as the parasitical poor, although in his article he stopped short of chopping hands from the gunwale. Hardin, retired from the University of California, writes today for *Chronicles*, a magazine published in Rockford, Illinois, which champions what it calls "Old Right" conservatism. In an article in the June issue, Hardin attacks the notion that we can continue to think that having babies is "a purely private matter" to be left up to parents. Decisions about what children should be born and how or whether "abnormal babies" should be cared for "are best made on the basis of opportunity costs to the community." All this is in the context of discussing national health care and the need to ration scarce medical resources. "A national health care system will be well justified," writes Hardin, "if it reinstates discrimination as a proper function of the social order." He wants it understood that he does not mean racial discrimination. The discrimination he has in mind is that between the fit and the unfit. He is not terribly hopeful that what needs to be done can be done. He writes, "The final solution (if there is one) is unknowable." Final solution? Final solution? Why does that phrase sound so familiar? (*November 1994*)

■ "The Politics of the Breast" is an opinion piece in the *New York Times* advocating the right of women to go bare-breasted on the subway. Two years ago the New York Court of Appeals ruled that the state laws against indecent exposure could not be enforced against women who wish to be topless in public. Judge Vito J. Titone wrote that differential treatment of female bodies violated constitutional guarantees of equality and was "rooted in centuries of prejudice and bias toward women." One suspects he meant to say against women. A certain delicacy about the display of the female body in public is indeed rooted, apparently from the beginning of the species, in an enthusiastic male prejudice and bias toward naked women. Such considerations seem to carry little weight with the court, however. If human nature and the edicts of the court are in conflict, human nature will just have to change. Mayor Giuliani, being a generally sensible fellow, says the transit police will continue to arrest bare-breasted women on the subway. A police spokesman explains that, in the close press of subway travel, a "very, very attractive" topless woman could create excitements that would pose a public danger.

Some subway patrons, he opined, could become so distracted that they might fall down escalators or even onto the tracks. The *Times* writer is buying none of it. She scoffs at the idea that "the power of the female breast is such that it can lure its beholders to untimely demise in subterranean channels." She concludes that the bare-breasted subway rider is making the point "that her breasts belong to her and not to the onlookers." It is not, however, the proprietorship but the public display of the items that is in question. To be fair to the writer, this is a man thing and it is perhaps understandable that she just doesn't get it. Her argument and that of the New York court, however, do helpfully illumine why it is so very difficult to make a case for public decency. The concepts of decency and indecency turn upon what is offensive. Today, unless you are a member of a certified victim group, you have not the right to be offended. If you are offended or, as in this case, aroused, the fault is with you. The fun for the more aggressive members of the certified victim group is to taunt and provoke you into protesting what they say or do, thus confirming that they are victims and you the victimizer. But this is old hat by now. And for all the media chatter about bare-breasted subway riders, we know nobody who has seen one to date. One expects it's not for the lack of looking. In any event, the ancient maxim is again vindicated that those whom the gods would destroy are, if madness be the sign, disproportionately New Yorkers. *(December 1994)*

■ We have a more extended comment on Gore Vidal in the works. But some of the comments on his *Live From Golgotha* are not without interest. This is the book in which Vidal presents Paul as the founder of a gay cult in which the genitally well-endowed Timothy plays a key role. Jesus, of course, is the fraud who founded a religion of "the skygodders" that has displaced the infinitely superior paganism embraced by Mr. Vidal. Alfred Kazin ended his review in the *New Republic* by suggesting that it is past time for Vidal "to just shut up." What apparently offended Mr. Kazin, however, was that Vidal had made an unfair remark about one of Kazin's academic friends.

Trashing Jesus and Christianity, it seems, is nothing to get upset about. A Random House advertisement for *Golgotha* quotes a *Newsweek* reviewer who said it was "bracingly blasphemous." One could hardly imagine Random House promoting a book as bracingly racist or bracingly sexist. Some sins are serious, and blasphemy is not among them. The same advertisement has another nice touch. The publishers obviously wanted a "banned in Boston" tag as testimony to the book's shock power. The best they could come up with was a statement by Bishop Michael Harty of Killaloe who said, "I will not read the book, and I will not spend money on it." Killaloe is in County Clare, Ireland. It strikes us that the publisher is desperately reaching to find evidence that Gore Vidal, at this late point in his decay, still has the capacity to outrage. Even the bishop of Killaloe sounds less outraged than uninterested. *(December 1992)*

■ Rabbi Joseph Gelberman used to be Orthodox and now he is Reform, of sorts. Once a year in his Interfaith Temple in Manhattan, on Valentine's Day, he does marriages free. All year round he declares that he is prepared to marry anyone— Jew, Christian, Hindu, gay, straight, believer, nonbeliever. The very genial rabbi says, "I'm not here to please God. I'm here to please God's people." As Aaron explained to Moses about the calf. *(May 1993)*

HOMOSEXUALITY AND THE CHURCHES

Rapidly changing attitudes toward Christian ministry reflect a cultural incursion into the life of the churches that is getting mixed reviews. In all the churches one hears seminary professors, bishops, and others in positions of oversight complain about candidates for ministry who are obsessed with careerism and self-fulfillment at the expense of discipleship and self-sacrifice. Others, acknowledging the change, say it marks a healthy step toward greater honesty, replacing the pietistic pretenses of the past.

John Cardinal O'Connor of New York recently pondered out loud about the need for a new order of sisters who would be vowed to poverty, chastity, and obedience and would have a special ministry to women with problem pregnancies and old people who (with reason) fear the implications of revived agitations in favor of eugenics. The *New York Times* picked up on the story and asked, among others, a Sister Ann Patrick Ware what she thought of the idea. She suggested that, to put it gently, the Cardinal is out of touch with contemporary realities. "The face of religious life is very different today," she said. "People are not about to take vows of poverty and chastity." The account did not explain why she did not include vows of obedience. Sister Ann Patrick, who coordinates a project called the Institute of Women Today, undoubtedly speaks for many in the ministries of the several churches.

The cultural pressure on traditional disciplines of ministry is evident on a number of fronts. The general challenge perhaps finds its most explicit expression in the proposal that the homosexually active should be fully accepted into the ministry of the churches. Here one discovers claims and arguments that extend far beyond the question of homosexuality. No "mainline" church formally accepts declared homosexuals in ordained ministry, except for the small and getting smaller United Church of Christ. Some observers thought the United Methodist Church might go along with the proposal, but in the last few years the tide seems to have turned against it. Homosexuality and ministry is a topic much discussed today, especially among Lutherans, Episcopalians, and Roman Catholics. Among Lutherans because the Evangelical Lutheran Church in America is a new jurisdiction of uncertain leadership that gay activists have been able to exploit to their advantage. Among Episcopalians because, for whatever reason and fairly or not, it is commonly believed that the Episcopal Church has an unusually high incidence of homosexual clergy. And, of course, among Roman Catholics, both because of the cultural stereotype that Catholicism is sexually repressive and because of the celibacy requirement for priests and members of religious orders.

Incidents and Incidence

Frequent news stories about scandals and lawsuits connected with priests doing naughty things with altar boys give the Roman Catholic situation high public visibility. But the issues joined in the Catholic discussion of homosexuality and ministry are not that different from discussions in other churches. Nor, for that matter, is it clear that there is a dramatically higher incidence of homosexual clergy among Catholics. Robert Nugent is a priest who heads up New Ways Ministry, an unofficial (and officially frowned upon) group that works with homosexual priests and religious. He notes that estimates of the percentage of homosexuals among male clergy "have ranged from the most conservative 10 percent to a more reasonable 20 percent or even 30 percent, although some have advanced estimates as high as 50 percent or more."

He himself gives credence to the claim that "20 percent of the clergy are homosexual and half that number are sexually active."

But these, to be sure, are nothing more than guesses, and they are guesses based on Kinsey's disputed claim that 13 percent of the male population is "exclusively or predominantly" homosexual. It thus appears that even those, such as Father Nugent, who have reason to accentuate the prevalence of homosexuality allow that the ratio of homosexuality in the priesthood is not that much higher than in the general population. Given the doubtfulness of Kinsey's data, and given the propensity of homosexual activists to count as a homosexual anyone who has ever had a homoerotic fantasy, it would seem that some media accounts of homosexuality and the Catholic priesthood are greatly exaggerated. To be sure, that is little comfort for those who believe that even one priest breaking his vow of celibacy, with a man or a woman, is cause for grave concern.

The campaign in the church for homosexual rights, as they are called, is by its own definition a frontal attack on church teaching and practice and on cultural patterns that the church is thought to have blessed in the past. *Homosexuality in the Priesthood and the Religious Life* (edited by Jeannine Gramic, Crossroad) is a useful guide to the campaign's developing attitudes, arguments, and strategies. It contains eight essays by proponents of a radically changed approach to homosexuality, and fourteen chapters of testimony by lesbians and male homosexuals in the priesthood and religious orders.

Self-declared radical Rosemary Radford Ruether asserts that "homosexuality is the scare issue in the Christian churches today." Not surprisingly, she portrays the assault in terms of self-defense. Homosexuality "is being used as the stalking-horse of all the current social fears concerning the disintegration of moral and social structures. We should see antigay fear and hatred as part of a cultural offensive against liberal egalitarian social principles generally. Homophobia is a vehicle for the conservative ideology that links the defense of the patriarchal family with the maintenance of class, race, and gender hierarchy throughout the society." Such a view, she says, is typically tied to "militarism and superpatriotism," and the whole thing has its roots in "patriarchal heterosexism." In this way, Ruether helpfully positions the campaign for homosexual rights at the center of the cultural war in which our society is embroiled. The battle in the churches is an extension of that cultural war but, given the role of religion in public life, it is also an effort to capture the churches' moral authority in that larger conflict. This strategic relationship between church and society seems to be well understood by the authors included in *Homosexuality*.

Understanding the Campaign

This book and similar literature display a number of arguments, perceptions, and attitudes that are important to appreciate if we are to understand a campaign that is likely to be with us for some time. First is the idea of the self and fulfillment. Second is the linkage between homosexuality and a comprehensive agenda of social change. Third, there is an inversion of the virtue of courage. Fourth is the redefinition of authority. Fifth is the conflation of civil and spiritual realms. Sixth is the notion of subculture as church. Seventh is the question of sexuality and personal identity. Eighth is the use and misuse of stereotypes. Ninth is the tension between fate and choice in homosexuality. Tenth is the perception of the sufferings of others. And eleventh is the connection between acceptance and forgiveness. Admittedly, that is a lot of points, and we will only briefly comment on and illustrate each.

On the matter of self and fulfillment, John Boswell, a Yale historian who has written some of the major texts employed by homosexual activists, asserts, "Not only is homosexual eroticism the oldest and most persistent strand in the Christian theology of romantic love, but Christian religious life was the most prominent gay life-style in Western Europe from the early Middle Ages to the Reformation, about two-thirds of the period since Europe became Christian." Here and elsewhere Boswell contends that today's negative attitudes toward homosexuality were not there in the Christian beginnings or in the first millennia. His arguments have met with considerable skepticism and resistance from other scholars, and the putative instances of homosexual relationships that he finds in the earlier period tend to underscore how very exceptional they were as a deviation from the norm.

But the more interesting point he seems to be making is that the monastic tradition, presumably premised upon self-denial, was an exercise in self-deception or conscious deception of others. Monasticism was in fact, Boswell suggests, a congenial way of life designed to accommodate the homosexual. The alternative possibility, that most monks would have adopted a life that got in the way of self-expression, and therefore self-fulfillment, is apparently not conceivable to Boswell's very contemporary mind. Similarly, other writers in *Homosexuality* insist that celibacy is appropriate only for homosexuals, assuming that "celibacy" does not preclude homogenital sex. (Andrew Greeley, on the other hand, has written that the tolerance of homosexuality among the clergy means that real celibacy, including abstinence from sex, is now being required only of heterosexual priests.)

The necessary connections between self-expression, self-fulfillment, and whatever counts as salvation are assumed in the homosexualist literature. An imperative external to the self that inhibits imperatives intrinsic to the self poses the threat of self-denial, which is the threat of death. So much, one might think, for the call to take up His cross and follow Him, except that several writers do compare the opposition they have encountered in their homosexual activism with the sufferings of Christ on the cross. (A priest celebrating a "liturgy for gay liberation" on the steps of the Supreme Court declares, "I offer up my body; I sacrifice my blood. I am consumed by a political system that refuses to liberate my sisters and brothers.")

A second striking feature in this literature is the linkage between homosexuality and a total agenda for social and political change. Daniel Maguire, a former priest who teaches theology at Marquette University, contends that discussions of sexuality ("pelvic theology," as he calls it) would not be nec-

essary in a "healthy" church. Such "micromorality" is a dis-
traction from the "macromorality" that focuses, for instance,
on the arms race and capitalism's oppression of the third-
world poor. Since most people apparently feel a greater sense
of immediacy about their sexuality than about, say, the international debt, Maguire's is a lone dissent among the twenty-
two writers in *Homosexuality*. For others, being homosexual,
and especially making a public issue of it, is the entree to a
culture of insurrection against the established order.

According to these writers, the established order is in very
bad shape indeed. In Ruether's view of a society captive to
heterosexist hierarchy, "it is as much a 'perversity' to be sexually attracted to persons of another race, religion, or social
class as to be attracted to persons of the same gender."
According to Ruether, people are not by nature either homosexual or heterosexual. "We are taught to become heterosexual," and to refuse to accept that teaching is to strike a blow
against an authoritarian social order. In a similar vein, Boswell
says that homosexuals are "outsiders," and as a consequence
are like "political dissidents in totalitarian regimes, Jews in
Nazi Germany, the left-handed in much of the world."
Typically, the writers affirm that, by virtue of their marginalization, they are in "solidarity" with other marginalized people. Homosexuality, if public and politicized, bestows the
moral status of being a victim. As one writer puts it, "I was not
black, or Chicano, or poor, or of the wrong social group—but
I was gay." This, he says, enables him to "confront the blatant
homophobia in my community, church, and society."

As was more general in the 1960s, "confrontation" is a key
component of homosexual activism today. It has been
observed that Oscar Wilde's love that dare not speak its name
has become the neurosis that doesn't know when to shut up.
But that misses the confrontational logic that requires "coming out of the closet" in a manner that forces reaction. If the
reaction is negative ("homophobic"), marginalization is
achieved, which brings with it both the desired victim status
and a vindication of one's claim that this is an intrinsically
hate-full and oppressive society. Some of the writers in

Homosexuality seem to believe that persuasion and "openness" can transform church and society, while others indicate that homophobia is so entrenched in the present order that nothing short of revolutionary apocalypse will do. But there is general agreement that being "honest" about one's homosexuality, which means making a public issue of it, secures one a position in solidarity with the oppressed and their agenda of radical change.

The Courage Claim

There is, third, the claim that these writers are being terribly courageous in talking about their homosexuality. The fact that eight of the twenty-two priests and religious in this book fear to write under their own names is intended to accent the threat posed by a homophobic church. If these writers are to be credited, the Roman Catholic Church in particular is afflicted by a fear and ignorance that impose a conspiracy of silence about sexuality, and especially homosexuality. Touchingly, if not believably, some writers claim that the conspiracy of silence was so complete that in their twenties and thirties they had not once heard homosexuality discussed, never mind homosexuality among priests or religious. Since it appears none of them were hermits or in secluded orders, one cannot help but wonder where they have been for the last twenty years.

"The present volume," the editor writes, "is intended to contribute to the further opening of the doors of silence that have blocked a healthy discussion of sexuality and homosexuality in some church circles." The reading of the book leaves no doubt that a "healthy" discussion is one that leads to "acceptance," and acceptance means agreement. The working assumption seems to be that a willingness to discuss homosexuality can lead to only one conclusion. A study guide on homosexuality that is officially promoted among Lutherans is titled, "Can We Talk About This?" It is premised upon the belief that talking about it is at least half way to agreement that traditional sexual ethics must be thoroughly revised. That others might study and discuss the issue and then arrive at a different conclusion is not admitted as a possibility. Another definition of courage—the courage of the dissident from the homosexualist position who risks being accused of homophobia—is not allowed.

Among Roman Catholics, Courage is the name of an organization for people of homosexual orientation who support one another in their efforts to live disciplined lives of chastity. In the dominant view of homosexual activists, however, Courage is anything but courageous. Not to give in to one's erotic desires, and not to declare publicly that one is doing so, is cowardly self-denial and, of course, an instance of homophobia. This curious inversion of the meaning of courage, once it is accepted, must be powerfully intimidating to those who might otherwise think they are called to resist courageously an impulse to sin. Further, we might normally think that engaging alternative viewpoints is a mark of courage, but not in this case. We are asked to believe that courage is the silencing of other viewpoints by peremptorily declaring them to be dishonest, unhealthy, and homophobic.

The fear of being accused of homophobia, what might be called homophobiaphobia, runs very strong in enlightened sectors of our culture. During last year's Gay Pride Week at Princeton University, the student newspaper declared that the suggestion that the merits of homosexuality might be open to critical discussion is itself an example of homophobia. Two years ago at the annual Erasmus Lecture in New York, Dignity, the Catholic homosexual-rights group, disrupted the meeting in an attempt to silence Joseph Cardinal Ratzinger, who had earlier dared to assert that homosexuality is "an objective disorder" that Christians should face with courage. So it seems that there may be a conspiracy of silence, but it is not necessarily located where the authors of *Homosexuality* claim to find it.

Then, fourth, there is the question of authority. Here we witness the rather thorough triumph of what Lionel Trilling many years ago described as "sincerity and authenticity" as the final court of appeal in "the adversary culture." Ms. Ruether, as might be expected, is quite explicit in advocating the displacement of tradition with her "revisionist" sexual ethic. Other authors, while clinging tightly to their "identity" as priests or religious, believe they would be guilty of complicity were they to work within the oppressive structures of the church. Assumed throughout is the "nonviability" of the distinction between the natural and the unnatural. The normal, defined in terms of what a person feels is normal, is the normative. Religious leaders must maintain the doctrines of the community, it is suggested, so long as such doctrines do not get in the way of the truth.

One way to get at the truth is through the *sensus fidelium*, the community's discernment of the truth. But the *sensus fidelium* to be consulted is the sense of those with immediate experience of the subject at hand—in this case, homosexuals. With respect to sexual ethics, it would seem that popes and bishops are excluded. "If the *sensus fidelium* means anything, it ought to be taken seriously by the bishops in this area in which they apparently have no direct experience," we are told. The conclusion is irresistible that, in the court of the adversary culture, the *sensus fidelium* cannot mean anything that might inhibit a person in the expression of his "true self." A priest writes, "One of the questions that inevitably arises is: why stay Catholic, and especially why remain a priest?" Despite the homophobia, he says he will leave the church one week after the pope does. "The Catholic Church is mine as much as it is Pope John Paul's or Cardinal Ratzinger's or anyone else's. My Catholicism is a deep part of my identity, as is my sexuality. I do not plan to give up either." In an intriguing inversion, the seat of authority is located in personal identity. One does not belong to a church because one adheres to its authority. In fact, one does not belong to a church at all. The church belongs to the supremely authoritative self.

Realms, Rights, and the Self

Also of interest, fifth, is the conflation of spiritual and civil realms. That is to be expected from a movement that has imported into the church our political culture's language of individualistic "rights." Blacks in society, we are told, have a right to have role models in positions of leadership, and it therefore follows that homosexuals in the church have a right to role models in the form of openly gay popes, bishops, and priests. The idea that individual identity should be subordinated to communal identity is viewed as intolerably oppressive—except, it seems, in the case of the "loving gay and lesbian support community." As the distinction between church and culture is collapsed, so also the public/private distinction must be overcome by "coming out of the closet." On the one hand, private behavior is nobody's business, least of all the business of church or state. On the other hand, what a person privately is and does must become everybody's business. Church leaders who care about justice will see that the gay-rights agenda prevails in the political arena, or at least will not oppose it. Cardinal O'Connor, a bishop whom the activists seem to love to hate, is guilty of opposing that agenda. This, writes one priest, reveals his inconsistency, if not his hypocrisy. "Cardinal O'Connor has not led a campaign to prevent divorced and remarried men from holding the office of President," he notes, presumably with reference to Ronald Reagan. It apparently does not occur to him that the rules and competencies appropriate to the body politic are different from those appropriate to the body of Christ.

With the conflation of church and culture, and with such a severely attenuated notion of what it means to belong to the church, one might conclude that the authors of *Homosexuality* have no church. It would seem, however, that at least for some of them their true church is the homosexual adversary culture itself. That culture maintains a number of "nurturing and networking" organizations, such as Dignity, Coalition for Catholic Lesbians, New Way Ministry, and Communication Ministry, Inc. Similarly, Episcopalians have Integrity and Lutherans have Lutherans Concerned. In the present volume there are repeated and sometimes moving narratives of a sense of "coming home" upon joining the homosexual community, much as Cardinal Newman and other converts have written about "coming home" when they joined the Roman Catholic Church.

One author tells how his priesthood took on "new dimensions" when he entered into "my Holy Communion with the lesbian/gay community." Participating for the first time in a mass sponsored by Dignity, "I knew that I had found my own people, a family that shared my particular crosses and that promised me a taste of resurrection joys." Here and elsewhere the dynamics and language are those of the sacramental rite of initiation. "Dignity," says this priest, "has been my most immediate experience of church." Another writer, a male religious in San Francisco, has apparently found not only the church but the kingdom of God: "So I have come to the 'new Jerusalem' with its wide open Golden Gate to complete the healing journey I embarked on many years ago."

Such expressions reflect a reconstituting of the world around the authoritative, and indeed authorial, self. But on the seventh point, having to do with sexuality and personal identity, homosexual activists appear to be of different minds. Boswell complains that homosexuals are treated unfairly when others think that their homosexuality is the most important thing about them. "In the case of a 'normal' person," he writes, "heterosexuality is assumed to be one part of his or her personality; in the case of a 'homosexual' person, sexuality is thought to be the primary constituent of his or her (abnormal) personality." Yet authors in the present volume repeatedly assert about themselves what Boswell complains is unfairly asserted by a homophobic society. "Being lesbian," writes a nun, "is my inner milieu, from which I relate with the world." About her "coming out," she explains, "I needed to reveal that most important part of myself that makes me 'tick.'"

It is not possible to explain the intensity of commitment that turns this movement into one's church apart from the primacy of sexuality in a person's identification of himself. Here we encounter a conundrum that has become familiar in the cultural wars. A just society, it is said, should treat a person as a person, not as a homosexual. At the same time, justice demands that society should come to terms with, and affirm, that person's homosexuality. We meet a similar, and similarly contradictory, construal of justice in some feminist literature, as well as in the claim that the society should be both color-blind and have preferential quotas for racial minorities. While many homosexuals are only asking for tolerance, the gay-rights movement is clearly engaged in a power struggle for the redesign of the social order. As in all power struggles, its antagonists need a public differentiation between "them" and "us," and in this struggle that makes inevitable the primacy of sexuality in personal identity. Thus it would seem that what Boswell and others attribute to society's prejudices is in fact the necessary logic of the movement they champion.

Stereotypes and Biology

The definition of allies and enemies unavoidably requires stereotypes. At one level, stereotypes are simply types that conform to a general pattern, but they are commonly much decried as a prejudice that unfairly puts people into preconceived slots. In gay-rights literature, and not least in *Homosexuality*, stereotypes play a dual role. They are fully engaged in portraying an often vicious picture of a society and church hatefully bent upon the persecution of homosexuals. At the same time, one encounters the stereotypes of homosexuals as unusually sensitive, creative, imaginative, playful, and loving. In short, stereotypes of homosexual superiority, or what is thought to be homosexual superiority, are not condemned but celebrated. In the present book, several male authors, reinforcing a stereotype, relate how in childhood they wanted to play house when the other boys wanted to play ball, and they were as a consequence called sissy, fag, and queer. This is told to illustrate the bigotry of their peers, but there is also a suggestion that a stereotype of deviant behavior must be flaunted if the movement is to achieve its goals. And this brings us to the question of fate or choice.

Gay activists commonly assert that homosexuality is biologically determined, and therefore nobody should be held responsible for his or her sexual condition. Typical is the priest who writes that "our journey has to be as sexual, as homosexual, persons. We have no other choice. God calls us to love and to celebrate who we are. He made us the way we are, and it is good." Others are not satisfied with this approach, however. They say it implies that homosexuality is a problem or handicap in which one has no say; it is a matter of fate. The implication is that the condition calls for sympathy from others. Rejecting that view, Rosemary Ruether joins Freud in arguing that we are all "originally" bisexual and polymorphously sexual. Against Freud, she contends that homosexuality is not an instance of arrested infantile or adolescent "perversity," but a choice for personal satisfaction and fulfillment. We should, she writes, "appropriate our sexuality not as something biologically necessitated, or as socially coerced, but as a freely chosen way of expressing our authentic humanness in relation to the special others with whom we wish to share our lives." The point is that people should not be held responsible for their sexual condition, for "originally" our conditions are the same. The further point is that people should not be held responsible for their sexual choices and behavior (at least not within the context of "a committed relationship"), for they are essential to "authentic humanness."

In this literature one is also impressed by the pervasive insensitivity and lack of feeling for non-homosexuals who experience discontents and sufferings related to sexuality. It appears that only homosexuals suffer. There is no mention of wives and husbands who, against powerful temptations and disappointments, strive to remain faithful to their marriage vows. Little credit is given celibates, of whatever sexual "orientation," who understand themselves to be offering up the entirety of their being to God. Indeed the logic of *Homosexuality* suggests that the difficult path of marital or celibate fidelity is a course of unhealthy denial and repression. Surely many married persons in the throes of temptation to adultery can (and do) claim that acting upon their desire is essential to their "authentic humanness." It is far from clear why intensity of desire comes with a moral license only for homosexuals. Advocates such as Ms. Ruether are at least more consistent in apparently extending the license to everyone.

In addition to being insensitive and unfeeling toward non-homosexuals who are coping with sexuality and its discontents, the activist literature is typically cruel and slanderous in its explanation of why most people have negative views of homosexuality. Anything other than the "correct" view of homosexuality is attributed to "homophobia," which is consistently described as the result of bigotry, ignorance, and the fear of one's own sexuality. If it is an instance of homophobia that parents earnestly hope that their children will not turn out to be homosexual, then almost every parent in the world is homophobic. Books such as *Homosexuality*, which incessantly talk about the fears, frustrations, angers, and depressions involved in being homosexual, inadvertently reinforce the reasons parents hope their children will not be homosexual. The dramatically higher incidence among homosexuals of suicide, psychological disorder, and sexually related disease (frequently lethal) suggests that homosexuality is anything but gay. Of course the activists blame these pathologies on society's intolerance, but it is not intolerance that produces another and very basic reason why people hope their children will not be homosexual. Whatever its alleged merits, homosexuality is sterile. Few things are more fundamental to societal interest and parental desire than the hope for children and grandchildren, for successor generations that will carry on our communal stories. The society's "failure" to put homosexuality on a moral par with heterosexuality is not a result of homophobia, as that term is now recklessly used, but of a human refusal to accept the end of history.

Acceptance, Not Forgiveness

Finally, one notes in *Homosexuality* an almost total absence of notions of sin and forgiveness. Sin is mentioned in passing as a hang-up of homophobes. One writer speaks of the experience of being "forgiven and accepted," but then makes clear that being "accepted" means that there is nothing to forgive. Several writers speak about how they and God feel good about their being gay, the implication being that "God" is some kind of cosmic concurrence in whatever makes human beings feel good about themselves. The Christian tradition's understanding of the ultimate inversion of "man turned in upon himself" (*homo incurvatus se*) is celebrated as salvation. "I am gay and happy; I am not neurotic, morbid, or maladjusted," writes one priest, protesting, one suspects, too much. "There are absolutely no apologies necessary," he asserts. What the tradition has viewed as disorder is in fact superior virtue, another writer declares. Homosexuals have "the ability to see with different eyes" and to "risk decisions which straight men and women, because of their greater stake in the dominant social system, cannot even consider." A lesbian nun writes, "I see myself as very much of a prophet among my own sisters."

Readers might be repelled by the tone of smug self-righteousness in *Homosexuality*, but that is to miss the underlying urgency in these assertions of self-approval, an urgency that betrays a terrible desperation. Some of the autobiographical sketches are touchingly ingenuous, revealing people who were hurt and confused in many ways and who then found the affirmation they were seeking in groups formed by sexual identity. Others border on the disingenuous, inventing comprehensive schemes of societal oppression which they blame for their unhappiness and which, simultaneously, they defy by flaunting their putative discovery of wholeness in their homosexuality. Some writers have the modest goal of integrating homosexual orientation into a life of celibate faithfulness. But the more frequently stated goal is as revolutionary as it claims to be—to displace the common wisdom regarding human sexuality in both church and culture.

This goal is evident in John Boswell's efforts to establish the marginal, the sometimes tolerated, and even the furtive on an equal footing with the Christian tradition. "Lesbian and gay religious need to reclaim their tradition, publicize it, rejoice in it, and share it with other Christians and gay people," he writes. "Models of gay Christian religious life embrace nearly every possibility of service to the Lord, from absolute chastity enriched by passionate attachment to another person, to open enjoyment and celebration of eroticism, to permanent unions, with or without physical sexuality. These models should be discussed and utilized as archetypes of Christian love. They are ancient, authentic, and as fundamental to the

Christian tradition as heterosexual marriage."

Homosexuality and the growing literature of which it is representative leave no doubt that the "acceptance" demanded from the churches is not acceptance as forgiven sinners. Traditionally, that is the only basis on which we are received into the community of the redeemed where we are sustained in the lifelong struggle against our devils, of which unruly Eros is by no means the most fearsome. What is now being demanded is not personal acceptance but agreement that Christian doctrine and morality are fundamentally in error. What is demanded is the formal blessing of libidinal liberation from communal restraints. Advocates of the movement disagree about whether sex should be within a "committed relationship," however defined, but are one in contending that what used to be called licentiousness must now be viewed as the freedom essential to fulfillment.

Homosexuality ends on the note that the revolution encounters growing resistance from church authorities. New programs are being introduced to screen out the sexually "disordered" among applicants for ministry. The implication is that, for all the homophile agitation, the homophobes may succeed in eliminating even the space that previously existed for deviance at the margins. Alarmed by the radical revisionism of the homosexual movement, it is suggested, the churches may be moved to reappropriate with vigor a traditional sexual ethic. It is a not entirely implausible prospect.

"Homosexuality is the scare issue in the Christian churches today," writes Rosemary Ruether. Nobody should deny that she and her companions in the cause are doing their best to make it sound scary. One can hope that the churches will decline to be intimidated by such scare tactics, remembering that antinomian challenges to the Christian ethic are nothing new. The current assault by homosexual liberationism should be countered firmly and lovingly by a renewed articulation of the rules by which we are to order our personal and communal life. That done, the churches can get back to their mission, offering God's forgiving and sustaining grace to all of us disordered and disorderly human beings who are subject to temptations beyond numbering, also in the realm of sexuality. (*May 1990*)

FT

WHY COMMUNISM COLLAPSED

The Soviet Union, we opined in the January issue, did not "collapse of itself"; a large measure of credit must be given to figures such as John Paul II, Ronald Reagan, and Margaret Thatcher. The Rev. Foster Freed of Knox United Church in Parksville, British Columbia, doesn't disagree, but he cautions that the way we put the matter could play into the hands of those who contend that there was nothing inherently wrong with communism. "Many on the left . . . are far from convinced that the fall of the Soviet Union proves much of anything. These folks invest a great deal of emotional energy waiting, on the one hand, for the advent of the next Nicaragua and breathlessly anticipating, on the other, the imminent collapse of Western-style democratic capitalism. They are only too happy to be told that the Soviet Union did not 'collapse of itself' but was undermined by some kind of sinister conspiracy, especially if they can associate that conspiracy with names like Thatcher, Reagan, and Wojtyla."

Mr. Freed expects there will be revisionist histories of the 1980s that will gleefully quote this writer in support of the argument that the problem was not with the Soviet system but with "external pressure orchestrated by the President of the only 'empire' they are ever likely to think of as truly evil." He makes a good point, in response to which this is an anticipatory disclaimer of any such revisionist misinterpretation. Could the Soviet system have stumbled on for another decade or two had there not been the pressures from the West? Scholars are not agreed on that, and we have no way of knowing for sure. In addition to the Western pressures there was, of course, the role of Gorbachev in launching economic changes whose political consequences he did not foresee. With respect to the internal crises of the Soviet Union, the most persuasive recent account we have read is David Remnick's *Lenin's Tomb* (Random House). The *Washington Post* correspondent in Moscow during the years of the collapse, Remnick depicts a level of mismanagement, irrational conflict, corruption, and mafioso-style gangsterism that makes the collapse seem all but inevitable.

So, it might be argued, to a significant extent the Soviet Union did "collapse of itself." At the same time, saying that leaves us with another problem. The revisionists whom Mr. Freed worries about can just as easily hijack the Remnick analysis, contending that the degenerate order he describes proves nothing about the merits of communism (or Marxist-Leninism, or socialism). The miscreants in charge whom Remnick depicts were, according to the revisionist script, traitors to the dream. For people of a certain ideological disposition, socialism is the name of their desire, and nothing can discredit that desire. Although expressing confidence in history's vindication of that desire, the desire itself escapes all of history's falsifications.

As for the collapse of communism, it happened as it happened. Hypothetically, it could have happened in a different way, or been delayed for a time. Ideological, economic, political, military, cultural, moral, and spiritual factors all played their part in what happened. For true believers, communism as a pure idea can never be discredited; but the real world does not allow space for pure ideas to work themselves out in a manner unaffected by everything else that is going on. In our view, Marxism-Leninism as an idea was a species of utopian madness, intellectually uninteresting in conception and necessarily brutal in application. It produced none of the benefits that it promised, and finally, it seems, was believed by almost nobody among those in charge of its implementation. It could not maintain its self-respect, it could not hold up its head, in the company of economic, cultural, and spiritual alternatives represented by figures such as John Paul, Reagan, and Thatcher. Posing as a great power is the last refuge of failed systems and, in view of the military challenge, the Soviet

Union could not any longer even claim to be a great power.

The humiliation was total and abject. And dangerous, as is evident in the political demagogues in Russia now exploiting the affront to Russian imperial pride. The surprises of history are such that we may soon wish that communism had collapsed in a different way. But the fact is that it collapsed as it did, by virtue of being a very bad idea in a world that refused to conform to its wishes. Of course, for those who thought it a good idea the fault lies with the rest of the world, and with the pseudo-Marxist managers who betrayed the dream. The socialist revisionists we will have always with us, for the desire becomes more demanding as the prospect of its satisfaction recedes. The idea, like a bird, escapes all the closing traps of historical fact. There must be, they insist, an alternative to this—to the paltry, striving, bourgeois, thus and so-ness of democratic capitalism. There simply must be. And there is of course. But those who do not know the alternative of a new heaven and new earth of ultimate promise have no choice but to cling ever more desperately to socialism as the name of their desire. *(May 1994)*

FT

SEARCHING FOR THE VITAL CENTER

E. J. Dionne, Jr. is among the most intelligent and fundamentally decent journalists in the major leagues today. Formerly with the *New York Times* and now with the *Washington Post*, he has written a book that has received, deservedly, wide attention. *Why Americans Hate Politics* (Simon and Schuster) is not for people who hate politics. It is an analysis of what has gone wrong over the last thirty years with our political culture. According to Dionne, the New Left that began in the 1960s entered a curious and inadvertent alliance with conservatism in devastating the liberalism represented by *The Vital Center*, published in 1949 by Arthur Schlesinger, Jr. Dionne wants to reconstitute that vital center.

In its lurch leftward, says Dionne, liberalism alienated "the restive middle class" and turned most Americans off politics altogether. Conservatives, especially the neoconservatives who emerged as a force in the late 1970s, capitalized on this alienation by waging war against government and, implicitly, against politics itself. There are many pieces to Dionne's argument, and they do not always hang together, but his basic point is that the kind of liberalism he wants to espouse now has the chance to return our politics to a more elevated form of democratic discourse. The chance is there, he believes, because conservatism has reached an impasse. The libertarian and traditionalist streams of conservatism that William F. Buckley and the *National Review* succeeded in patching together for a long time are now breaking apart.

Dionne makes a great deal of the much-publicized clashes between paleoconservatives and neoconservatives. The traditionalist paleos declared open war on the neos over many questions, but the split became most evident in the reemergence of right-wing isolationism during the crisis in the Gulf. One suspects Dionne makes much too much of these little wars. There is columnist Pat Buchanan, but then it is hard to name even three or four other opinion makers with any kind of national constituency who fit the description of paleoconservative. The notion that conservative ranks are deeply split and the conservative movement has come to a screeching halt is dearly cherished by those who, like E. J. Dionne, long for the reappearance of a liberalism with which they can identify without embarrassment.

All who esteem republican virtue and democratic discourse must share Dionne's desire for a politics that rises above the frequently nasty left/right polarizations of recent decades. He describes his book as "an inchoate demand . . . for an end to ideological confrontations that are largely irrelevant to the 1990s. It is a demand for steadiness, for social peace, for broad tolerance, for more egalitarian economic policies, for economic growth. It is the politics of the restive majority, the great American middle." Wishing, however, will not make it so.

Dionne has a remarkably benign view of the forces that are chiefly prosecuting the cultural wars that he deplores. For instance, this on feminist and homosexual activisms: "Feminists demanding equality for women were not selfish souls who put the children second; they were rational human beings responding to a world that had been vastly transformed, and to which they wished to make their own contribution. Gays demanding tolerance were not looking to insult the heterosexual world; they were simply asking that they not be picked on, ridiculed, and discriminated against." But surely Mr. Dionne is familiar with the declared purposes of NOW and Act-Up, just for starters. There undoubtedly are feminists and gays of more moderate disposition, but it is folly to overlook the impact of movements that are utterly serious in their outspoken determination to effect cultural revolution. And it is passing strange that Dionne, whose chief political concern is for the Democratic Party, tends to downplay the degree to which that institution is in deep hock to the most extremist sectors of those movements.

Dionne recognizes the shadow cast over his wistful hope for a kinder and gentler politics by the question of abortion. "If any one issue is obstructing the formation of such a center, it is abortion." His solution? "The right-to-life movement needs to accept that its primary task is not political but moral." With stunning understatement, he observes, "Accepting that abortion will remain largely legal indefinitely is not a happy prospect for the right-to-life movement." Of course the prolife movement is not about to accept that. Suggesting that a political and cultural struggle be resolved by one side giving up its cause is not likely to prove very persuasive. To be sure, the pro-life movement is about much more than politics, but in a democracy such as ours political struggle is itself a potent instrument in advancing the moral education for which Dionne rightly calls.

Every student of Aristotle, Locke, or Burke will readily second Dionne's call for a more elevated public discourse. Yet democracy is now and always has been a rough and raucous process. Like Dionne, we may well deplore the money and media nexus that dominates political campaigning while, unlike Dionne, we may also believe that very substantive questions about the common good were joined, for instance, in the 1988 contest between Bush and Dukakis. We may not like it, but our society is engaged in a *Kulturkampf*, a war over the values, symbols, and truths by which we ought to order our life together. Behaving in as civil a manner as we can muster, we will just have to see the conflict through.

One wonders if E. J. Dionne and many like him are valiantly resisting the recognition that they are neoconservatives. Almost all that he endorses—the critique of current liberalisms, the affirmation of family and republican virtue, the importance of mediating structures in redesigning social policies, the embrace of bourgeois values, the need to include the marginalized in the mainstream of economic productivity, the leading role of America in international affairs, the critical significance of religion in public life—are planks, so to speak, in the neoconservative platform. Maybe someday the vital center for which Mr. Dionne yearns will once again be called liberalism. Maybe the insistence of Dionne and others that they really are liberals will help that to happen. Who knows? But for the present and foreseeable future that vital center is called neoconservatism. Labels aside, however, *Why Americans Hate Politics* is an engagingly wise analysis of what happens when political schemes are divorced from moral foundations. *(August/September 1991)*

FT

WE SUPERIOR FEW

"Radicals are the ones who first protest, liberals are the ones who join them when their protest has begun to be heard, and conservatives accept or at least live with what the liberals finally win." So far Joseph Fletcher, he of "situation ethics" fame, in a autobiographical sketch written shortly before his death in 1991. When he was young, he was "an ideologue and doctrinaire, which took shape in two guises, Socialist and Christian. The first to die out was the socialism, then the Christianity." What never died out was the smugness, although he does not put it quite that way.

Looking back on his contributions to biomedical ethics, he writes: "I have seen legal and medical triumphs for such 'radical' innovative practices as artificial insemination and inovulation, in vitro fertilization (test tube babies), genetic engineering, brain-death statutes, germ and embryo freezing, the patient's right to know, transsexualization, and DNA splitting and recombination. We have won the wars for voluntary abortion and sterilization and will soon have completed the roster of states with right-to-die laws. All these things and more, in both categories, were radical by definition and by general sentiment, and yet all of them have been won. Let it not be said that radicals are ineffective—only that they tend to pay a lot personally for what they gain, as liberals do not—at least comparatively."

Not, in fact, that Mr. Fletcher, a comfortably ensconced Episcopalian clergyman (which he remained to the end of his life, long after his Christianity "died out") and tenured professor at the University of Virginia, ever had to pay that much for his radicalism. Of his life he writes: "It was good, all of it. I knew many people, of all kinds and stations, in many parts of the world; had an exciting intellectual life, a superb family; lived in pleasant homes almost always, some of them beautiful; and our children had the great advantage of top-grade schooling and friends."

The above is from *Joseph Fletcher: Memoir of an Ex-Radical*, a new book of essays in appreciation of Fletcher edited by Kenneth Vaux and issued by Westminster/John Knox Press. Fletcher's putative achievements in biomedical ethics are by no means so secure as he assumed. And, far from having the courage to be radical, his life's work was one of going with the flow of technological ambition and moral permissiveness. His autobiographical reflection confirms the impression of an affably arrogant man who was born to a life of privilege and security and never had the wit to recognize that he had cast his lot with the barbarians who were willing to make him a minor celebrity in exchange for lending his prestige to their project of destroying the world from which he so richly benefited. May God have mercy on his soul. *(June/July 1994)*

FT

A PALEOLIBERAL CREED

The following excerpt from an essay they published is cited by the editors of *Commonweal*, the liberal lay Catholic magazine, to promote subscriptions. Presumably, it represents the spirit of what today is meant by Commonweal Catholicism. Readers can readily substitute Baptist, Episcopalian, Lutheran, or whatever, for the word Catholic. The essay, by Nancy M. Haegel, is a rather touching affirmation of an older form of liberalism, by no means dead, that is deserving of careful attention.

> As Catholic Christians, we embark from
> an immense tradition of belief,
> and yet it is only that—an embarking point.
> Ultimately, we must each call
> upon our own individual experience.
> I have had just enough of what
> might be termed "religious experience"
> to entice, startle, and intrigue me.
> Just enough so that
> I can never deny it, but not
> so much that I don't wonder,
> in an expression I heard somewhere,
> why "God is so damn subtle."
> So if my work colleagues
> know that I am a Catholic,
> they know that I am

a doubting and tolerant one,
believing in a God
who is merciful with our doubts
and prefers them
to our certainties.

Note, first, that the "immense tradition of belief" is only prelude. Paul, Irenaeus, Gregory of Nyssa, Augustine, Catherine of Sienna, Thomas Aquinas, all the way through von Balthasar—it is all an embarking point, and "only that." An embarking point is what you leave behind, it is what you are freed from in order to get on with—what? Why, with ME, with "our own individual experience." That experience, we are told, entices, startles, and intrigues. The question of truth does not arise, at least not directly. Her own experience is strong enough that she cannot deny it, but not so strong that she does not wonder. Presumably, strong conviction, even conviction about one's own experience, is the enemy of wonder. God is indeed often subtle, all must agree, but the point of Christianity is God's revelation of himself. Revelation does not figure in this creed, unless "individual experience" counts as such.

"So if my work colleagues know that I am a Catholic . . ." *If.* It is not the kind of thing about which one is public in these very secular times, don't you know. It is not the kind of thing that is so important a part of me that anyone who knows me would know it. But if, despite all, they do happen to find out that I am Catholic, "they know that I am a doubting and tolerant one." A convinced and faithful Catholic, it is suggested, would likely not be tolerant. Catholicism wholeheartedly embraced, it follows, is intolerant. No anti-Catholic, or anti-Christian, could have put it more succinctly.

From, presumably, the revelation of her individual experience, she has learned to believe "in a God who is merciful with our doubts and prefers them to our certainties." The God of biblical revelation is certainly merciful with our doubts, there is no doubt about that. But he prefers our doubts to our certainties? God is, we are asked to believe, displeased with St.

Paul's "I am persuaded" (Romans 8) or a congregation boldly asserting, "We believe in God, the Father Almighty . . ." And is the only thing exempt from Ms. Haegel's doubt the certainty that God prefers doubts to certainties? How on earth did she arrive at that certainty, which she seems not at all to doubt?

The paleoliberal creed puts one in mind of Chesterton's remark about an absolutely open mind being like a constantly open mouth, never able to come down on anything solid. This affirmation, which *Commonweal* offers as representative of its editorial posture, calls for a tentative, timorous search for truth in the understanding that truth—truth for sure—is not to be found. It is an embarrassed Catholicism. "Yes, I admit to being a Catholic, but, despite that, I am not (fill in any caricatures of Catholics that come to mind)." It is the creed of apologetic Christians that has given apologetics a bad name.

Finally, we are glad to say that the editors of *Commonweal* are wrong. Ms. Haegel's creed is not representative of the magazine today, which is with growing frequency feisty, assertive, self-critical, and unapologetic about being Catholic. The fact, however, that the editors would lift such a vacuous essay from the past to sell their wares indicates that the paleoliberal fever has not been definitively shaken. Pray for continued recovery. (*August/September 1993*)

FT

STARTING FIGHTS

"As some tell it, religion wasn't a big issue in this comfortable, ethnically diverse Buffalo suburb until last fall. Then the school board unveiled a new policy to help children get along better." So begins a *New York Times* story about Williamsville, New York. And wouldn't you know it, the program to get along better, like the New York City program to teach "tolerance" of homosexuality, soon had everybody, including the children, going for the jugular. The brilliant Williamsville idea, hardly original, was to pretend that the majority of people who live there are not Christians, and therefore to put down any "privileged" references to Christianity.

"Handel's 'Messiah' could be performed as long as there was no audience sing-along and the music of other religions was mixed in for balance," reports the *Times*. A little Hari Krishna chant, perhaps, just before "I know that my Redeemer liveth." We are further informed, "The North High School's annual Christmas Concert was renamed the Winter Concert, but it still featured a Christmas tree and a visit by Santa Claus." Well, as long as they keep the essentials of Christmas.

What madness this all is, and it is happening all across the country. And what just madness it provokes from ordinary folk who know perfectly well that almost all of them are Christians, or at least claim to be so, and the only way to "get along better" with fellow Christians and others is to draw on, not deny, the religious and moral teachings that they embrace. Tolerance is not a free-standing virtue. Why should an overwhelming majority of Christians be tolerant of Jews, Hindus, Muslims, or atheists? Because otherwise the minorities will be unhappy? "Tough," is one answer to that. Because otherwise, given the nature of this democracy, society will be thrown into civil commotion? That's somewhat more serious, but majorities have been known to dispense with democratic niceties.

The reason Christians are tolerant is not because this is a pluralistic society. This is a pluralistic society because most Christians are tolerant. And they are tolerant for Christian reasons—because they believe that everyone is a child of God, that consciences are not to be coerced, and even terribly wrong opinions are to be tolerated out of respect for the human dignity of those who hold them. Christians have not always understood the imperatives of tolerance, and some on the Christian fringes still don't. But what the ACLU, the National Education Association, and their like must some day learn is that the only available reservoir of public morality in this society is the dominant ethos, and that dominant ethos is, however confusedly, Christian.

Absent that understanding, any program to help people get

along better is sure to set them to fighting. Admittedly, some people think that is a big plus. Says Margaret Mendrykowski, chairman of the Williamsville program, "I think the issues were there. Any time we unearth issues of prejudice and misunderstanding and work on them, it's positive." The alternative view is that there are very sensible reasons for keeping prejudice and misunderstanding well buried. It is sometimes called repression, without which no civilized order can survive. When nastiness comes to the surface, it must be addressed in a morally explicit way, but it is never wise to go poking around in search of potential nastiness. Not recognizing that, the progressive campaign in America is bent on turning public schools and other institutions into anger factories of civil discontent. (May 1993)

FT

THE UNCLOUDED ACADEMY

At the University of Toledo, a state university, a chair in Catholic thought has been established through private funding. It has stirred something of a brouhaha. The university newspaper huffs: "UT President Frank Horton recently said this is the 'first endowed professorship in Catholic thought at a public university in the United States.' This just may be because other public universities in the United States have refused to sell professorships in any religious discipline in order to maintain a curriculum rooted in objective thought, unclouded by religious beliefs of any kind." The paper's eagerness to preserve the unclouded discourse of contemporary academe is touching.

The Ohio ACLU finds the precedent "troubling" but notes that the chair is only for electives and therefore "there's not as strong a case for an establishment clause violation." The ACLU spokesperson continues, "If it's true that the course need not be taken by any student at UT in order to obtain his or her undergraduate degree, there is a much lesser element of coercion." As, for instance, in none at all. An alumnus grumbles in the newspaper that you can't believe the claim that the chair will not be used for proselytizing. "Five of the instructors are Catholic priests. How can they present Catholicism in an unbiased manner?" The alumnus should be reassured by the knowledge that among the five priests who will serve as initial lecturers are Fathers Richard McBrien, Richard McCormick, and Arthur McGovern, none of whom is thought to be excessively biased in favor of official Church teaching.

If the Catholic chair is allowed, opines this unhappy alumnus, "Even humanists and atheists may establish professorships." We, too, would find it strange if in the contemporary university humanists and atheists had to resort to private funding and limit themselves to elective courses. The question, of course, is whether Catholic thought or, for that matter, Protestant or Jewish thought is a subject worthy of attention in higher education, and, if it is, whether it can only be taught by people who are certified as not believing in what they teach. As the ACLU and its like never fail to remind us, the price of maintaining the wall of separation between education and the university is, like that of liberty itself, eternal vigilance. (*August/September 1992*)

FT

WHILE WE'RE AT IT

■ In another publication we recently did a whimsical little piece occasioned by a politically correct manifesto issued by The Magickal Childe, a Manhattan store specializing in things demonic. In response to which comes a blast from one who styles himself as "The Reverend Peter H. Gilmore, Administrator, Church of Satan." He is unhappy with us for many reasons, not least because our article suggested that

Satanists, proponents of goddess worship, and neo-pagan stone fetishists are all part of the same phenomenon. Doctrinal distinctions are in order, according to the Rev. Gilmore. "In fact, these so-called 'pre-Christians' reject any connection with Satan, and rightly so as they share the appalling doctrine of altruism espoused by Judeo-Christian and humanist 'thinkers.' Satanism rejects these idealistic and unnatural creeds to embrace the world as it is: a ground for endless strife and struggle, a total war wherein the strong dominate the weak and the clever dominate the strong. We Satanists are our own Gods and consider Satan to be a symbol for the carnal nature of Man unleashed, as well as the dark force which permeates all of existence and fuels the evolutionary advancement of life itself." Now if only more of our churches were so clear about what they stand for. *(November 1992)*

■ The autobiography of Father Theodore Hesburgh (well not quite "auto," since it was written "with Jerry Reedy") is titled *God, Country, and Notre Dame* and is reportedly selling briskly. The dustjacket is carries this blurb from the *Washington Post* review: "Fascinating . . . Engaging . . . The man is a wonder-worker, a Catholic version of Averell Harriman or George Ball—the man popes and presidents call upon when things get stuck." We would in charity, like to think that Father Ted is not responsible for the dustjacket either. *(January 1992)*

■ Among the most infamous of Nazi war criminals was Dr. Josef Mengele. At Auschwitz he was known as the "Angel of Death" for his lethal "scientific" experiments on prisoners. After the war, the Angel of Death escaped to Argentina where authorities have now opened the files on Nazis who found refuge there. It turns out that Mengele made his living in Argentina as an abortionist. It figures. *(June/July 1992)*

4

THE MANY CAUSES OF ENVIRONMENTALISM

The Woodstock Center at Georgetown University is where some distinguished Jesuits, and some less distinguished Jesuits, fiddle with their theological fretwork. A recent *Woodstock Report* is entirely given over to fretting about today's favorite crisis, the environment. It comes with a recommended bibliography of seven books, topped by Matthew Fox, *Original Blessing: A Primer in Creation Spirituality*. The book is described this way: "Going beyond systematic theology, Fox sets forth the ingredients of a *spirituality* that would make us more sensitive to the sacramental character of nature. His major thesis is that theology's over-emphasis on the Fall-Redemption schema has led us unnecessarily to deny the basic goodness of Creation. Though the book is considered controversial and one-sided by some critics, Fox's is a voice that needs to be heard today."

The "Fall-Redemption schema," of course, has to do with that business about our being sinners for whom Christ died. Fr. Matthew Fox, it will be remembered, was silenced by the Vatican last year, which prompted him to take out a full-page ad in the *New York Times* soliciting funds for his projects in cosmic synthesis and christic witchery. "I HAVE BEEN SILENCED!" he announced. But the gimlet-eyed Jesuits are surely right in seeing that his theology is not systematic. Whether it is Christian is . . . well, who is to say these days?

One vaguely remembers the time when "Jesuitical" suggested something more sinister than silly.

Admittedly, the sinister and the silly are not mutually exclusive. In times of desperation, the most dubious purposes can continue to be advanced under the banners of myriad fatuities. After the demise of Marxism as an ideological force, and the severe body blows dealt to schemes of socialist "third ways" propounded by "prophetic" religion, the banner of choice is currently THE ENVIRONMENT. Thus the huge confab of the World Council of Churches in Seoul, South Korea, titled the "World Convocation of Justice, Peace, and the Integrity of Creation." And thus the gathering at Riverside Church in New York City this past May, "National Conference on Building the Earth Community."

The last was a grand reunion of veterans of the tattered causes of the last several decades, except now under the rallying cry of the environment. Peace-and-justice networking, Third World liberationism, radical feminism, unilateral disarmament, socialist utopianisms—there is little substantive change but, by scissors-and-paste magic, all the speeches and manifestos begin and end with alarums about ecotastrophe. The standard polemics against capitalism, imperialism, racism, militarism, and whatever are now marginally recast in terms of the supposed threat such evils pose to Our Planet—or, as it is now said, "The Earth Community." Such ideological cross-dressing is not surprising. True, yesterday's arguments sometimes look a little odd in today's fashion of environmentalism, but then one remembers that the alternative would be a perhaps painful reexamination of assumptions to which many have attached their identities. As with the Old Left of the thirties, so with the New Old Left of the sixties, it is ever so much more important to "keep the faith" than to think clearly about a changing world.

Then too, religionists of a certain proclivity have a touching need to believe that they are in some important way making history. From almost any source they eagerly embrace the assurance that they can be relevant to "the real world." And so the Riverside conference headlines the assurance of celebrity astronomer Carl Sagan, who says that "scientists and the religious community must work together to preserve the environment of the Earth. The historical record makes clear that religious teaching, example, and leadership are powerfully able to influence personal conduct and commitment." Sagan is outspoken about his adherence to atheistic materialism, a belief system that, however implausible, he has every right to promote. The remarkable thing is that Christians and Jews should feel complimented when he pats them on the head by admitting that their religion is nonetheless useful in changing the world. He does not go so far as to say that religion is a noble lie, but he is prepared to acknowledge that it is a useful lie. That is enough for him to be gratefully applauded by religionists who are thus reassured that they still have a role to play, no matter how modest, in making history.

These are among the dynamics that account for the crowding of the environmental tent with the refugees from causes past. But, in addition to finding an ecological preservative for ideas fast spoiling, and in addition to the need for comforting assurances that religion is still relevant, environmentalism offers new "spiritualities," and for new spiritualities there is today a bull market. On our discontents with ourselves, others, and the world, on our fears about the future, eco-gurus offer to rub the balm of essence of soul. Jay McDaniel, author of *Earth, Sky, Gods, Mortals: Developing an Ecological Spirituality*, was featured at Riverside, and the books of the aforementioned Matthew Fox were much in evidence.

Again, none of this should surprise us. Aging activists need a temporary home, a place to keep their weary dreams for a time, before continuing the sojourn toward a world that is the more alluring because it is so elusive. The Environmental Rest Home will have to do for a while. The young who want revolution grasp at the promise wherever it is on offer, even if the revolution, ironically enough, is in the cause of conservation. As for the quest for spiritualities, it is a perennial eruption in human history. Robert Musil, in *The Man Without Qualities*, noted its eruption in the useless lives of the elites of Vienna prior to World War I. In that time, as in ours, there was what

Musil says was an "indescribable wave of skim-romanticism and yearning for God that the technological age had for a time squirted out as an expression of spiritual and artistic protest against itself." (*August/September 1990*)

FT

NOTES ON THE CULTURE WARS

Almost nobody wants to be called a prude and reactionary, a bluenose puritan and spoilsport. It would not be accurate to say that nobody wants to be perceived that way. Some, when they have been called reactionary once too often, embrace the epithet and exult in it. When he launched *National Review* thirty-five years ago, William F. Buckley wrote that its purpose was to stand athwart history and yell Stop. As it turned out, *National Review* did not stop history or even slow it down. It has had a powerful influence on changing directions that our several establishments had declared to be inexorable. Nonetheless, most people do not share Mr. Buckley's relish for a fight. They prefer to identify themselves as "moderates" safely situated between "the extremes." Just as they would not be viewed as prudes or reactionaries, they definitely do not think of themselves as libertines or revolutionaries. The culture wars have everything to do with defining the extremes.

There is little doubt that recent decades have witnessed a distinctly conservative shift on many political and economic questions. Socialist bromides and the notion that human problems can be resolved by government programs are ideas that have been, at least for a time, discredited. Support for market incentives and the empowerment of people to control their own lives is no longer thought to be reactionary. On the contrary, it is generally recognized that those two components are at the heart of truly progressive thinking about society. To be sure, such progressive thinking is today often called conservative, but that only means that conservatism has become "the smart party," while its opponents seem to be mired in the failed programs and tired slogans of the past. Not for nothing has liberalism become a term of opprobrium. One may have some sympathy for those who insist that their version of "authentic liberalism" has not been tried yet, but their complaint is inescapably touched by a tone of desperation.

The political and the economic are important, and those who call themselves conservative can take considerable satisfaction from the trends of the last three decades. Of course their cause was mightily boosted by the Revolution of 1989 in Eastern and Central Europe, a revolution that exploded socialist utopianisms quite beyond the force of all the arguments, exposes, and polemics fired since 1917. Beyond the political and economic, however, is that comprehensive and often vaguely understood sphere that we call the cultural. Culture is conventionally discussed in the puffball terminology of "values." More substantially, it has to do with shared convictions about what is right and what is wrong, what is noble and what is base, what is decent and what is obscene. Compared with politics and economics, culture is thought to be the "soft" dimension of public life. Quite the opposite is the case, however. Politicians appear to be engaged in gaseous abstractions and economists in the reading of entrails compared with the immediacy and consequentiality of questions cultural.

Culture is the way we live, and the way we live in argument with the way we think we ought to live. It has to do with what we eat, wear, watch, admire, and abhor. It has to do with dating, and marriage, and raising children, and trying to get a grasp on what it means to live a good life before our lives are over. These, as any sensible person knows, are the hard questions. A sensible person is here defined as one who immediately and without further explanation recognizes the truth of Dr. Johnson's observation, "How small, of all that human hearts endure,/That part which laws or kings can cause or cure."

For sensible people, whether the Fed raises the interest rate or there is a Democratic majority in the Senate pales in importance by comparison with whether Junior is on drugs or his father is seeing that other woman. This testifies to more than the truism that the personal is more important to most of us than the general. (Although many people have been convinced, apparently, that what is in the morning headlines somehow matters more than how they are living their own lives.) The point here is that the general reality called the cultural has a greater impact, for better and for worse, than the general realities called politics and economics. Admittedly, we are speaking in general. If the politicians stumble into world war or the economy nosedives into deepest recession, the impact upon the personal can be impressive indeed. Barring those extremities, however, how we live our lives and how we think we ought to live our lives—i.e., the cultural—is of premier importance.

Evidence of a Conservative Shift

Now a case can be made that also in the realm of the cultural there has been a conservative shift over the last three decades. The contrast with the 1960s is instructive and not altogether unencouraging. Most of the countercultural liberationisms of that time are now viewed as silly and destructive by all but the silly and destructive tenured professors who never tire of retelling the bliss it was to be alive and young in the Age of Aquarius. Consider the drug culture. Then the term was associated with the adventuresome and the chic. Now it denotes, almost without exception, the desperation of wasted lives in the urban underclass. The swingers, the singles bars, the open marriages—all are now consigned to a sordid past. For the most part.

In case after case, the counterculture has been effectively countered. Or so it would seem. Marriage is back, and it is by no means unfashionable to say a good word for fidelity. Women who were once persuaded that they could "have it all" are recognizing that choices must be made, and a growing number make no apology for choosing home and children. Making it in the male world increasingly seems less an achievement than a confinement. To be sure, at the margins the feminist battles are still pressed. There was a great fuss and flurry about the woman reporter demanding her right to hang out in the football locker room. "A woman's place is any place," the *New York Times* sententiously opined. More sensible people laughed and allowed as how it was best to leave the boys to their games.

There are other positive indications. Having rediscovered the merits of marriage, an increasing number of very bright young people have hit upon the idea that marriage and children seem to go nicely together. We will not be surprised if very soon the statistics indicate that the "birth dearth" has bottomed out. In all our years in New York, we have never seen so many prams on the street, or so many women looking quite pleased about being expectant. (That is anecdotal information, admittedly, but then real life is mainly anecdotal.) For all the sadness attending the black underclass in our cities, the awareness of the phenomenon seems to have made it the conventional wisdom again that, without marriage, stable families, and regular work, life is likely to turn into an awful mess. That that wisdom was for a time unconventional is an indication of how determined some were to blind themselves to the obvious.

In addition, it seems that we are on the edge of being able to talk again in public about public decency. Oceans of ink have been spent on the controversy over the National Endowment for the Arts and its funding of what most sensible people think to be pornography, albeit sometimes very "artistic" pornography. While the Congress will extend NEA for a time, the champions of its old ways can take little comfort from the legal restraints placed upon its libertine propensities. The cant and clamor about censorship and First Amendment rights notwithstanding, it has penetrated even most political minds that there is something not a little outrageous about expecting taxpayers to put up the money for "art" that is expressly intended to outrage them. If people insist upon taking pictures of men peeing into one another's mouths, they should do it on their own dime, and preferably behind closed doors. Most Americans would rather not know about it. They are reluctant to send in the cops, but neither do they want to pay for activities that, try as they might, strike them as per-

verse. It is one of the happy failures of our educational system
that it has not succeeded in persuading normal people that
there is nothing abnormal.

And so it would seem that, on several cultural fronts, we
are witnessing a veritable renascence of common sense. In
addition to the evidences above, there is much discussion of
how those who were dismissively called yuppies are now
returning, or turning for the first time, to religion. On the
most fevered of moral issues in public, namely abortion, there
is an expanding consensus that the question is how and when
the unborn should be protected by law, rather than whether
they should be protected at all. Put it all together, and one can
make an impressive case that there is underway a popular, and
possibly long-term, shift toward cultural conservatism, or, as
some might prefer, toward the perennial wisdom about how we
ought to live together once the subordinate questions of politics and economics have been settled.

"Progressive" Enclaves

Just when you thought it was safe to go out again, enter
developments to the contrary. Perhaps they are not so much to
the contrary as they are simply complicating developments. The
liberationisms of the sixties are thriving, and in fact becoming
more aggressive, in some sectors of society. Notably in the universities, more "progressive" church circles, and the communications media. These, as scholars have explained in great detail,
are the chief dens of "knowledge class" iniquity. These are the
kingdoms of the experts, the domains of people who are paid to
know. And one thing they know for certain is that any opinion
that is popular is almost sure to be wrong. Their calling is to take
the unpopular side, and they boldly do so, especially when taking any other side is, within their little worlds, dangerously
unpopular. That is why intellectuals and would-be intellectuals
are described as a herd of independent minds.

For a while, and this was not without its embarrassments,
it seemed that the knowledge class had prevailed. As with
prophets of whom all speak well, there is an awkwardness
when elitists are popularly acclaimed. But the rewards made

up for the awkwardness, and we were for a decade and more presented with the declared triumph of "the greening of America," the arrival of "Consciousness III," and other cultural transformations of the bad, uptight (remember uptight?), oppressive way that—or so it was said—America used to be. The jargon of cultural revolution that now seems so quaint was very much preoccupied with sex. The protagonists of the counterculture had sex on the mind, which, as Chesterton observed, is a very unsatisfactory place to have it. They still do have sex on the mind.

The afterglow of the cultural revolution that failed is, as noted earlier, burning brightly in the little worlds of liberal religion. Those worlds are becoming littler year by year, but those in charge of them claim not to he fazed. This, they say, has always been the fate of prophets who keep the faith. A different dynamic is at work in the communications and entertainment media. They are, after all, commercial enterprises. ABC and CBS must remain at least within hailing distance of the popular mood if they are to sell the advertising that pays the bloated salaries of its so very progressive stars. The prospect of boycotts and sponsor cancellations has a wonderful way of concentrating the mind. The universities, the third institutional refuge of radicalisms past, are not similarly inhibited. Buffered by endowments, tax funds, an inflexible tenure system, and the aura of academic freedom, they are free to impose the party line of yesteryear's liberations until the retirement of the last professor who lives his life in nostalgic remembrance of being briefly alive at Woodstock. What were once cultural eruptions are now ossified in quotas, entitlements, and rules against free speech that violates politically correct opinion. Pondering the place of universities in our culture, Chester Finn aptly describes them as islands of repression in a sea of freedom.

Yet Another Force

In addition to these three institutional homes for the refugees from radicalisms past—the churches, the media, the universities—there is another force that seems to be increasingly aggressive. Moving beyond the three enclaves of countercultural shelter, homosexual activism is a growing factor in our politics, especially in urban politics. In San Francisco and New York, of course, but not only there. In the view of many, the cause of "gay rights" is very much on the ascendancy. It is joined by radical feminism but, within the movement itself, it is recognized (and much lamented by the feminists) that the women are something of an appendage. Lest there be any misunderstanding, we are speaking of *radical* feminism; that is to say, women who make no secret of the fact that they do not like men, that they view the institution of marriage as a kind of incarceration, and that they consider heterosexual intercourse to be tantamount to rape. Such radical feminists are, as often as not, the admittedly lesbian adjunct to gay activism.

Movements for women's rights, taking on various hues of radicality, are nothing new. They have been coming and going for at least two centuries. Women's movements come on as a fundamental challenge to the gender-related institutions and habits of the ages, and then recede while consoling themselves that they have attained a greater measure of equality. Homosexual activism is something new. What started twenty years ago is unprecedented in our cultural history. The homosexual movement is inherently and of necessity fundamental in its challenge. Unlike feminism, it cannot settle for adjustments in the relationships between women and men within the institution of the family.

The organized homosexual cause has no choice but to be at war with those relationships and with that institution. In the past, homosexuals, if they were known as such, hoped to be viewed with tolerance as a relatively harmless exception or even deviation from the norm. Today, to "come out of the closet" is to declare war on the norm. And those who refuse to come out on their own are increasingly being publicly exposed (it is called "outing") by activists who declare war on their behalf. The challenge is unquestionably fundamental. It is a challenge both to the majority culture and to the previously discreet subculture of the "gay world," the existence of which cosmopolitans have always taken for granted.

By the early seventies, homosexuality had hitched a ride with the civil rights cause. Now everybody was a victim, everybody claimed to be the "nigger" of societal oppression. Remarkably enough, the civil rights leadership welcomed gay activists as allies, thus endorsing the inevitable blurring of the specificity of race-based grievances. The gay activists no longer demanded tolerance or a tacit acknowledgment of their "lifestyle" in a pluralistic society. Everything must now be made explicit. Past habits of homosexual discretion were now condemned as betrayal. The wisdom of La Rouchefoucauld, that hypocrisy is the homage that vice pays to virtue, was repudiated. The cry went up, No more hypocrisy! Hypocrisy would be ended not simply by vice refusing to pay homage but by vice demanding to be accepted as virtue.

In the late seventies the push was on for "gay rights bills" around the county. Many communities resisted. In New York the resistance was led by the Roman Catholic archdiocese and Orthodox Jews, and a gay rights bill was not passed until 1986. Such bills focused on prohibiting discrimination in housing and employment and most Americans, being Americans, thought that fair enough. The late Paul Ramsey of Princeton was among the few in mainstream Protestantism who argued publicly that such gay rights bills were a ruse. They were not aimed, he contended, at remedying an injustice but at redefining justice. Justice, according to the proponents of such bills, requires that the society be prevented from publicly indicating its preference that people deal with their sexuality in a manner supportive of family and children. When accused of being anti-family, the gay activists and their allies protested vigorously, while at the same time engaging in an intensive campaign to "redefine" family out of existence. That campaign reached its apogee in the ill-fated White House Conference on Families under the auspices of Jimmy Carter.

The Critical Wedge

That Paul Ramsey and other critics were right is now evident to all who have eyes to see. Far from being the pathetic victims of discrimination, homosexuals in our major cities are among the most affluent and influential of citizens. This should come as no surprise. Well-educated professionals with no dependents have an extraordinary advantage in discretionary time and income. The reality has not been lost on politicians and businessmen in our urban centers. Were homosexuals the victims of discrimination, one would have expected an upsurge of housing and job complaints after the passage of gay rights bills. In fact, that has not happened. The gay rights bills were important for a quite different reason. They were a critically important wedge, opening the way to additional steps in relativizing the social and moral status of heterosexuality and the family.

The additional steps followed quickly. Some cities and university-dominated small towns have arranged for marriage-like registrations of homosexual partnerships. New York State has decreed that such partners are entitled to inherit rights to rent-controlled apartments. Employers are being successfully sued for death benefits coming to the "spouse" in a homosexual relationship. Mayor David Dinkins of New York boasts of the number of lesbians he has appointed to family courts. Dinkins has articulated the grand vision. Addressing the Gay and Lesbian Alliance Against Discrimination last spring, he noted that, "It's the media that shapes the attitudes that prevail in our culture. . . . Where are the gay characters on TV sitcoms? Why are there not more lesbians on soap operas? When will there be an out-of-the-closet commentator or anchor on national television or on the local news?"

Giving the lie to the notion that homosexuals are denied access to housing or employment, Dinkins goes on: "Gays and lesbians serve in government, as teachers, as police officers, as corporate executives, and they ought to stand prominently and proudly in the media spotlight as well. Only then will the fact of homosexuality become an accepted part of the reality of America, a real land of liberty in which you ought to be able to hold hands without fear of assault, or kiss your lover goodbye without worrying about who is watching." What must become "an accepted part of the reality of America" is that discretion is no longer required in departing from the assumed normality of male-female relationships. In that ideal world, presumably, there would be no Greenwich Village, for the dominant "lifestyle" of the Village would be the at least equally accepted lifestyle everywhere. Probably closer to the reality, the goal is to somehow force the working class boroughs of Queens and Brooklyn to publicly approve of Greenwich Village.

That goal is not easy to achieve. Perhaps because they recognize that, gay activists have become ever more desperately aggressive. Act-Up, among the most strident organizations, has regularly disrupted services at St. Patrick's Cathedral, in one notorious instance breaking up a mass and desecrating the consecrated elements. Queer Nation is the name of a militant group that aims to force the majority to accept homosexuality by reverse epithet, much as some militant blacks call themselves "bad niggers." A few years ago it was declared a great victory when the city went along with reverse discrimination, opening a high school just for more aggressively homosexual students.

Of course readers may think, with some justice, that New York has always been more than a little crazy. With respect to homosexuality and other "alternative lifestyles," New York and San Francisco constitute a two-ring circus that the rest of the nation watches more with amusement than alarm. True, New York remains, for better and definitely for worse, the cultural and media center of the nation, indeed of the world. Its influence on Duluth and Dubuque cannot be dismissed lightly. That said, however, homosexual activism here may have gone as far as it can go. In this connection, New York may be more the backwater than the avant garde. Most cities cannot muster the "critical mass" of homosexualism that makes this circus possible. New York may well reduce the homosexual influence in Duluth and Dubuque by serving as a magnet that draws gays who want to act up in the big time. And political clout, as represented by David Dinkins, could be shakier than it appears. His administration is in hopeless shambles and it seems likely that he is a one-term mayor. So maybe this most publicized assault on the family by homosexuals and radical feminists should be no great cause for concern within the national context of a culture sobering up after an extended liberationist binge.

Paying the Price

Nonetheless, serious damage is being done. As usual, the price is being paid by those least able to pay it. In New York City, that means the black and Hispanic children caught in the financially bloated and educationally decrepit public school system. The school bureaucracy, cheered on by gay activists, has announced its intention to distribute free condoms in the high schools, and maybe in the junior highs. This is advertised as a campaign to reduce the incidence of AIDS by encouraging "safe sex." The message could not be clearer. It is that teenagers among the poor are incorrigibly rutting animals incapable of taking charge of their lives. The message is also that the schools must be "value free" with respect to sexuality. There must be no hint of censure, nor the slightest suggestion that one way is better than another. Fornication, adultery, and, of course, homosexuality are but different ways of seeking the sexual satisfaction to which we are all entitled. Each has its own way of "bonding," and results in its own kind of "family." And, needless to say, we "value" family very highly indeed.

These programs are sold under the label of public health. This despite the fact that study after study over the last fifteen years has shown that value-free sex education, combined with access to contraceptives, results in an increase rather than a decrease of adolescent sexual activity, venereal disease, and teenage pregnancy. Nonetheless, educational authorities keep a straight face while declaring, among other things, that the way to reduce AIDS is to teach children that homosexuality is an equally "viable" form of sexual expression. Critics say that homosexual activists press for the promotion of homosexuality in the schools in order to bend young people of an impressionable age toward their "lifestyle." We might hesitate to judge motives, but one reality is beyond reasonable doubt. The same programs and propaganda would not be tolerated in the schools of the middle class and affluent. The children of the underclass are a captive audience, in the fullest sense of "captive."

They have no choice. They have to go to the schools that everybody else has abandoned. They are the ones who are left. They are the guinea pigs of the cultural revolutionaries who have been rejected by the larger culture. In communities of the black underclass, where over the last quarter century the institution of the family has for all practical purposes disappeared, children are taught about the oppressive nature of the "nuclear family" that they have never known. Their teachers and textbooks sneer at the "Ozzie and Harriet" families that will, just as the teachers and textbooks say, remain for these children always a "myth." It is an unspeakably cruel thing to do to little children.

Such, then, are notes on the culture wars. In the economic and political spheres, there are heartening signs of something like a turn toward sanity. Similar signs are evident in the culture. Sinecured silliness holds broad sway in the mainstream churches, in the universities, and in the media. What used to be the mainstream churches are drying up; the media, however reluctantly and erratically, adjust to their markets; and tenured professors will one day die, making room for a generation that is not prepared to spend its years living in the afterglow of youthful radicalisms. There is reason to be hopeful about the future. Except for the captive children of the underclass. They will continue to be the victims of the cultural revolutionaries from whom the larger society has turned away in disgust. (*January 1991*)

FT

THE LAST PRIESTS

"I have ability, creativity and imagination in an organization that doesn't value those qualities." That is Father Richard McBrien, former head of theology at Notre Dame, a Catholic university in Indiana. He is speaking about the Catholic

Church. The statement is typical of those to be found in forty-two interviews included in *The Last Priests in America: Conversations with Remarkable Men* by Tim Unsworth (Crossroad). McBrien admires Father Charles Curran, another Catholic *enfant terrible* who has troubles with Church authority. "We need people in this Church," says McBrien, "with voices like Charles Curran's—and mine—who are committed and yet willing to say: 'This is not right!'" What McBrien has in common with almost all of those interviewed is the conviction that he is vastly superior to the Church that he putatively serves.

There are exceptions. Among the better-known exceptions are Monsignor Jack Egan and Joseph Cardinal Bernardin of Chicago, and J. Bryan Hehir of Georgetown University. They speak movingly of the burdens and blessings of being a priest. They and two or three others do not belong in this book. *The Last Priests* is, for the most part, a collection of bitter, even bilious, commentary by aging men looking back on misspent lives in an institution that, they are convinced, was not worthy of their talent or devotion. It is a rambling, repetitious book, apparently printed without benefit of research or editing. (The author seems not to know whether the encyclical *Humanae Vitae* was issued in 1965 or 1968. It was 1968.) It is a very sad book. The stories told are hardly representative of the Catholic priesthood today. Mr. Unsworth writes for *National Catholic Reporter*, a kind of *National Enquirer* of American Catholicism, and he has chosen to interview those who follow its endlessly reiterated line that the Catholic Church is headed for oblivion unless it restructures itself in a manner reminiscent of liberal Protestantism. Most of the interviewees are indeed "the last priests" of a style of priesthood that gained prominence in the 1960s.

A Grim, Bitter View

Unsworth and his conversation partners raise repeated alarums about the decline in vocations to the priesthood. One can hardly imagine a document better calculated to discourage young men considering that calling than *The Last Priests*.

Many of those interviewed were, a few still are, parish pastors. To hear most of them tell it, parish ministry is the pits. Among evangelical Protestants today there is much excitement about "megachurches," congregations of two thousand or more members. There are several dozen of them around the country. Of the 19,000 Catholic parishes in the U.S., the *average* number of parishioners where there are two or more priests is well over two thousand. Parishes that have six or seven thousand people at Sunday masses are not unusual. Yet there is no similar excitement among the priests with whom Mr. Unsworth talks. On the contrary, there is a thinly veiled, and sometimes nakedly revealed, contempt for the people and piety of the Catholic "system." In place of a sense of responsibility for ministering to the faithful there is the relentless complaint that the priesthood stifles the exercise of the "ability, creativity, and imagination" that these men allegedly have in abundance.

In American culture during the 1960s the habit took hold of blaming "the system" for every discontent public and private. In the sector of the priesthood examined by Mr. Unsworth, as in the fetid groves of academe, the habit has not been kicked. His priests indulge in unrelieved self-pity about their noble visions that were frustrated by a recalcitrant Church. Dysfunctional men who resigned the priesthood in order to marry, who wrecked their ministries on the rock of alcoholism or drugs, and at least one who served time for sexually abusing a minor; all rail against what they describe as a "dysfunctional Church." The priest convicted of sexually abusing a boy complains of the ill treatment that he and other sex offenders received in jail. He protests the injustice of it all: "The boy I was accused of abusing was practically a grown man, for God's sake." Another homosexual priest who is HIV-positive says, "What would I say to the Church? I'd tell them to grow up." Presumably he knows all about growing up.

Unsworth calls his priests "remarkable men," and they are that—for their superficiality, for their utter lack of introspection or self-reproach, for their unexamined confidence that their grand visions would have produced a lovely Church and world, had they not been foiled by an ecclesiastical system controlled by vile and stupid reactionaries—with John Paul II and Cardinal Ratzinger being at the top of the list. This pontificate is compared to Soviet totalitarianism. Andrew Greeley, the sociologist and pulp novelist, is among those who make that comparison. "We could have a Gorbachev in the Church," he says. But he is doubtful about that happening, for, as a friend told him, "the bishops simply don't have enough nerve or enough courage."

Sex on the Mind

Most of the interviews are preoccupied with celibacy, married clergy, and the need to ordain women. These are veritable obsessions, and are proposed as the key to almost everything. One priest who resigned his ministry declares that "the Church can't have any real significance until it gets honest about celibacy, women, and the pill." There is the repeated charge that celibacy is "only for heteros," that homosexual priests can hang out and sleep together with impunity. There may not be that many homosexual priests, but it is another convenient stick with which to beat the celibacy requirement. The connection is made between celibacy and clericalism. Almost all those interviewed condemn clericalism as a very bad thing. None, including Mr. Unsworth, notes the irony that this book is patently an exercise in clericalism. The author and his remarkable men assume the mystique of the priesthood—a mystique not entirely unrelated to celibacy—even as they dismiss that mystique as magic. One cannot imagine a comparable book of interviews with malcontent United Methodist ministers, or with unhappy dentists. Here are priests deriding the priesthood even as they insist that attention be paid because they are priests.

One says the priesthood is "an aberration." Others opine that the Church, and perhaps the entirety of Christianity, is an aberration. Harvey Egan was pastor of a large parish in south Minneapolis and exults in being called "Harvey the Heretic." He is, we are told, a "skilled infuriator" who invited such as Philip Berrigan, Robert Bly, and Gloria Steinem to speak in his parish. He is a very bold man. "[Richard] McBrien is one of my heroes," he says. "Our parish property became a nuclear weapon free zone, but it didn't seem to make a differ-ence." Apparently nobody wanted to launch or drop a bomb there anyway.

Now retired, Egan looks back on a progressive priesthood in which progress is measured by making the priesthood obso-lete. "Hans Küng raises the question of what happens when Christians get together," he says. "Does anything happen? He believes that it does. But do we need the priest? Parents can do baptism. In Penance we can ask God for forgiveness. Confirmation can become a Bar Mitzvah. In Matrimony the priest is only a witness and the perpetuity of marriage is being reconsidered. Extreme Unction has been long under scrutiny. Do we need a grease job at the end of our lives? It's the direc-tion of our lives that really counts. And so it gets down to the Eucharist and one must ask: Is it really necessary to have a priest for Eucharist? The priesthood could disappear." In fact it is not clear why all those rites, including the Eucharist, should not disappear, since they are depicted as vestigal tribal habits of what Andrew Greeley calls "communal" (as distinct from doctrinal, liturgical, or ethical) Catholics.

After a Long, Long Run

Harvey Egan's reflection captures nicely why Unsworth's remarkable men are not the last priests in America but the last priests of a certain kind. They are the priests who championed an uncomplicated convergence of the Second Vatican Council with the spirit of the time known simply as "the sixties." In fact, it was not a convergence but a collision. The Council was the fruition of decades of *ressourcement* in theology, biblical studies, liturgy, and pastoral teaching. It was aimed at bringing the defensiveness of the Counter-Reformation to an end by reappropriating the riches of the Great Tradition to which the Catholic Church lays claim. Unsworth's remarkable men, by way of contrast, viewed the Council solely in terms of *aggior-namento*—of "updating" the Church by bringing it into sync with the cultural revolutions of the sixties.

From the wreck of the collision between Council and

Zeitgeist, these priests and theologians picked up pieces of the Council that fit their progressivist agenda, and indeed tried to hijack the Council itself in the name of "the spirit of Vatican II." At first hesitantly under Paul VI and then energetically under John Paul II, the Church began to take back the Council. That project of reclamation and repair is now far advanced and shows no sign of flagging. It is little wonder that these last priests, who now know that they are the last priests of their kind, speak with such anger and bitterness.

For others of that generation, it is less anger than dismay. They seem not to understand why the project of deconstructing the "system" must itself deconstruct. The books of one interviewee whom Unsworth calls a "clerical prophet" sold big in the fifties and sixties. He strikes a rare note of something very near to self-reproof. "I had a constituency in those days," he says. "Now, my constituency is gone. . . . The liberal Catholics of a few decades ago had a network throughout the country. Now, there's no such group. Future chroniclers will not speak fondly of us. We have not prepared the next generation of ministers. We could have had an orderly transition. Instead, there'll be nothing to pass on."

A similar note is evident in the reflection of William McManus, retired bishop of Fort Wayne-South Bend, in which Notre Dame is located. Richard McBrien thanks Bishop McManus for protecting him from the alleged reactionaries in the Church. McManus, on the other hand, wonders if he did not miscalculate what was happening in those years of progressivist "renewal." Speaking of the tightly structured seminary where he received his formation, he says, "I was so glad to be free of the place that, even years later, as a bishop, I thought that I had done my duty by simply telling my priests that they were free to develop their talents. 'You're free!' I told them. That didn't encourage them. They hadn't come from such a structured past." Precisely. Being told that one is "free to be" is not very encouraging when one has no idea what he is free to be, as most of the remarkable men of *The Last Priests in America* obviously have no idea of what it is to be a priest. The meaning of a life spent in getting liberated from a structure cannot survive liberation. Freedom is an empty achievement if there is no answer to the question, Freedom for what?

Meanwhile, thirty million or more Catholics in the U.S. go to Mass every week, the morale of the faithful and most of the clergy is palpably reviving, the drop in vocations to the priesthood has bottomed out, and there is a slow but sure recovery of doctrinal and moral coherence. Today's seminarians shake their head in wonderment at an older generation that saw it as their mission to dismantle the Church that they, who are aspiring to the priesthood, are resolved to serve.

Off on the sidelines, in the ruins of a failed revolution, surrounded by a few aging and dispirited comrades, superannuated leaders poutingly protest, "I have ability, creativity, and imagination in an organization that doesn't value those qualities." Mr. Unsworth seems to think that they are the prophetic vanguard. Those who understand what has happened gently reassure the last priests of their kind: Yes, yes, you really are able, creative, and imaginative, but now your act is over, the curtain has fallen, and it is time for you to shuffle along. A new and quite different drama of Catholicism in America has already opened. The show called "The Sixties" closed some time ago. You should not feel so bitter about it. It had a very, very long run. (*March 1992*)

FT

COUNTING ANTI-SEMITES

Sorry, we know that some of you are tired of the subject, but in this kind of world anti-Semitism is a question of continuing importance. The Anti-Defamation League (ADL) has once again taken a survey that it first used in 1964 and reports that at present 20 percent of Americans are anti-Semitic. How do they arrive at that conclusion? Anti-Semitism is measured by the response to eleven propositions. Those who say "probably true" to six or more are counted as anti-Semitic.

The eleven propositions are: (I) Jews stick together more than other Americans; (2) Jews always like to be at the head of things; (3) Jews are more loyal to Israel than America; (4) Jews have too much power in the U.S. today; (5) Jews have too much control and influence on Wall Street; (6) Jews have too much power in the business world; (7) Jews have a lot of irritating faults; (8) Jews are more willing than others to use shady practices to get what they want; (9) Jewish businessmen are so shrewd that others don't have a fair chance in competition; (10) Jews don't care what happens to anyone but their own kind; (11) Jews are not as honest as other businessmen.

The measurement is questionable on several scores. Seven of the assertions are undoubtedly negative. Assertions 4, 5, and 6, however, are very close to being redundant. Number 7, the assertion that Jews have a lot of irritating faults, strikes us as true of any group of people we know, including Jews. Moreover, three of the other propositions might be construed as positive characteristics by many, if not most, Americans. That Jews stick together, are ambitious, and are exceedingly shrewd in business might well be said admiringly. In our experience with Jews and non-Jews, these things frequently are said admiringly—and, by non-Jews, with a touch of envy. Were such things said of Italians, would anyone think it defamation? People who belong to some other ethnic or racial groups can only wish that the same could be said of them. Of course those assertions are also amenable to a negative construction, and maybe that is what most respondents had in mind. But they are very doubtful criteria by which to measure anti-Semitism.

The ADL report says that "the number of Americans within the 'most anti-Semitic' segment has declined slowly—down only 9 percentage points in twenty-eight years—from 29 percent in 1964 to 20 percent in 1992." In addition to the doubtfulness of the measuring instrument, one may be permitted to wonder whether, in the larger scheme of historical change, a one-third decline in less than thirty years is all that slow. Further, the report notes that most of those counted as anti-

Semitic are older—over 65 years of age—and have a high school education or less. Nonetheless, the head of ADL declares, "It boggles the mind that in 1992 a significant segment of American society has bought into the classical canards and stereotypes that allege Jewish power. It is distressing that the stereotypes so alive in the 1930s, which led to horrific consequences, did not die in the ashes of Europe, but have found a rebirth in America today. We find it to be sinister and dangerous."

More careful reflection might conduce to an unboggling of the mind. The power and influence of Jews in American life is not merely "alleged." The observation that Jews, who are 2 percent of the population, exercise an influence vastly disproportionate to their numbers is not based upon canards and stereotypes but on a reasonable awareness of the success of Jews in academe, the media, entertainment, business, science, and other centers of societal potency. Whether one thinks that that power is "too much" may indeed have something to do with anti-Semitism, but to deny its existence is to insult the intelligence of Americans, Jewish and non-Jewish alike, and to invite suspicion of those who do the denying.

Anti-Semitism is not finding "a rebirth" in America today. By ADL's own, and almost certainly inflated, figures, anti-Semitism is declining, and dramatically so. Most of those counted as anti-Semitic are old people hanging on to vestigial prejudices. However doubtful the survey's methodology, ADL may be justified in worrying that black Americans are more than twice as likely to show up in the "most anti-Semitic" category than whites—37 percent to 17 percent. But even if we credit the accuracy of the data, that is clearly a deviation from the pattern. There will always be a certain number of people who really don't like Jews, just as there will be those (often the same people) who have a generalized dislike of other groups. But the reality is that, far from being reborn, anti-Semitism is dying in America. And none too soon. *(March 1993)*

No Valentines For Jesus

We shouldn't be surprised, but we still are from time to time, by evidences that most Americans are happily ignorant of continuing threats to the free exercise of religion. John Whitehead is founder of the Rutherford Institute, a Virginia-based civil liberties organization that is tirelessly in the trenches fighting on behalf of ordinary folk who are told that they are constitutionally required to keep their religion to themselves. Whitehead has written an extremely useful book on how these questions are joined in the schools. It is called *The Rights of Religious Persons in Public Education* and is published by Crossway Books in Wheaton, Illinois.

In Hartford, Wisconsin, a teacher urged third-grade pupils to "be creative" in making valentines to be displayed in the school hallway. One eight-year-old was apparently too creative, scribbling on her valentine, "I love Jesus" and "Jesus is what love is all about." The teacher said her valentine could not be displayed because of the religious message. The principal and superintendent backed the teacher, until Rutherford threatened a lawsuit. In Norman, Oklahoma, a half-dozen eleven-year-olds used their free time during recess to read the Bible and pray. Horrors! said the principal, who informed their parents that such religious practices are illegal. Rutherford is in court on that one. In Oswego, New York, a high school student was told that he could not perform his Christian "rap" routine in the school talent show. The superintendent relented after Rutherford intervened. Rapped Kenny Green: "My name is Kenny Green, and I'm a Jesus machine. I love Jesus Christ for he is not mean. I became born again at the age of fourteen." Kenny received a standing ovation. (Score one for religious freedom, and one for the awfulness that is rap.)

In a number of municipalities, prolife groups are prevented from putting up their materials on public bulletin boards because it is "too controversial."

Rutherford, with ACLU-like relentlessness, is on the scene, breathing threats of lawsuits right and left. Whitehead notes that many school districts continue to resist the Equal Access Act, passed by Congress seven years ago and upheld as constitutional by an 8-to-1 vote of the Supreme Court. Some officials have threatened to close down all non-curriculum-related student clubs rather than allow a religious club (an action unfortunately permitted by Supreme Court guidelines). In Philadelphia a teacher can be fired for wearing "any dress, mark, emblem, or insignia" of religious significance. And so it goes.

These are little matters, you say? Tell that to James Madison or Roger Williams. The right to believe what one will and to bear public testimony to that belief cuts to the heart of the American experiment in a free and just public order. It is never a little matter for those whose freedom of religion and conscience is being trampled. We do well to remember that the freedoms we tend to take for granted are, in disputes all around the country, being defended daily by organizations such as the Rutherford Institute, the Christian Legal Society, the Catholic League for Civil and Religious Liberty, Dean Kelley of New York and William Ball of Harrisburg, Pennsylvania (each of whose prodigious energy is tantamount to that of an organization). Except for the rare fracas that catches the eye of the press, their work goes essentially unnoticed. So we thought it an appropriate time to take note, and say thank you. (*November 1991*)

FT

APOLOGIZING FOR THE FAITH

We were in Canada at the time, where the statement received enormous attention from the media. It touches on events also in this country having to do with the 1992 observance of the arrival of Europeans in the Americas. There are 1,200 members of the Missionary Oblates of Mary Immaculate in Canada. On July 24, the order officially issued "An Apology to Native

Peoples." Apparently, the Oblates have much to apologize for. In recent years there have been much-publicized incidents of the sexual abuse of boys and girls in Oblate schools. The schooling system itself, set up in the last century, tore children away from their families in, as the statement puts it, an "attempt to assimilate aboriginal peoples." The July apology, however, goes far beyond practices that are clearly to be apologized for.

"As large-scale celebrations are being prepared to mark [1492], the Oblates of Canada wish, through this apology, to show solidarity with many native people in Canada whose history has been adversely affected by this event. Anthropological and sociological insights of the late-twentieth century have shown how deep, unchallenged, and damaging was the naive cultural, ethnic, linguistic, and religious superiority complex of Christian Europe when its peoples met and interrelated with the aboriginal peoples of North America. . . . We recognize that this mentality has from the beginning and ever since continually threatened the cultural, linguistic, and religious traditions of the native peoples."

The missionary enterprise was one of "systemic imperialism," the 3,000 word statement declares. Reflecting on their own history, the Oblates acknowledge the "many men and women, native and white alike, who gave their lives and their very blood in a dedication that was most sincere and heroic." Sincere and heroic, but utterly wrongheaded. The statement says it is "honoring" these people "despite their mistakes" and "the past blindness" of the order. It concludes with solemn pledges of reform: "We want to denounce imperialism in all its forms and concomitantly pledge ourselves to work with native peoples in their efforts to recover their lands, their languages, their sacred traditions, and their rightful pride. . . . Despite past mistakes and many present tensions, the Oblates have felt all along as if the native peoples and we belonged to the same family." The Oblates declare that they "renew the commitment we made 150 years ago to work with and for native peoples," and they do so "in the spirit of our founder, Blessed Eugene de Mazenod, and the many dedicated missionaries" of the past.

The statement, which we would like to think does not

reflect the views of all the members of the order, is noteworthy in many respects. It gives a quite new meaning to "apology for the faith" (as in *apologia*). One might also note the irony of using ideas that are undeniably constructs of Western culture—solidarity, anti-imperialism, self-esteem, the universal family of humankind, respect for pluralism—to condemn the influence of Western culture. If imperialism means, as the statement suggests, challenging ideas and patterns of behavior with other ideas and patterns of behavior, "An Apology to Native Peoples" is an instance of thoroughgoing imperialism. It is a frontal assault on the constituting ideas of the Christian missionary enterprise (including, of course, the original enterprise of the Oblates) and could hardly be more alien to thought patterns indigenous to the native peoples of this continent. The statement perfectly reflects the mindset that John Murray Cuddihy brilliantly analyzed in *No Offense* as "the Protestant etiquette" that is determined not to raise awkward questions that might make others uncomfortable. The etiquette itself, of course, offends those who believe that ideas have an uncomfortable way of making a difference.

A Yet Greater Betrayal

Most notable, however, the statement not once mentions God, Christ, the Gospel, the sacraments, saving grace, or eternal life. "Anthropological and sociological insights of the late-twentieth century" have presumably demonstrated that it is not true—as Eugene de Mazenod and his colleagues undoubtedly thought it was true—that Christ is Lord and Christians are to be in the business of calling others to faith in Him. The Oblate statement repeatedly puts "cultural, linguistic, and religious traditions" in the same category and on the same level. The Oblates apologize for the missionaries having "threatened" those traditions. But of course the assertion that Christ is Lord "threatens" the religion of those who do not think Christ is Lord. It is a cognitive challenge, it can be painful, it gives offense. One way to avoid the challenge, the pain, and the offense is simply not to assert that Christ is Lord.

The Oblates declare their rejection of "the premise that

European languages, traditions, and religious practices [are] superior to native languages, traditions, and religious practices." But if the Mediterranean (not European) message that the God of Abraham, Isaac, Jacob, and Jesus is the one true God is not "superior," in the sense of being true, one must wonder what is the mission of the *Missionary* Oblates. One might also wonder what the many Native Americans who converted to Christianity think about now being told that they were cruelly duped and should have stayed with their indigenous beliefs. Having abandoned the Christian mission, the Oblates "pledge to native peoples our service." They acknowledge that they are not sure what that means. "We ask help in more judiciously discerning what forms that service might take today."

Admittedly, 1492 and its consequences is a subject riddled with moral ambiguities. The question of missionary encounter with non-Christian cultures and truth claims is also, as it is inevitably said, very complex. Those complexities are imaginatively addressed by Pope John Paul II in his recent encyclical on missions (*Redemptoris Missio*). The Oblate statement takes the cheap way out from such complexities by embracing a thoroughly "European" brand of mindless relativism. Among Catholics today, and especially in various aging religious orders, there is interminable discussion about the "crisis of declining vocations." The truth must be told: Young men and women are not inspired to commit themselves to communities that do not deserve their commitment—to communities that do not themselves know what they are committed to. It is very hard to imagine people giving "their lives and their very blood in dedication" to a community that, in a posture of abject self-denigration, is sniffing around in search of "what forms its service might take today." Without reference to Christ and the Gospel, bland chatter about Christian mission is simply pathetic. It would seem that the Oblates, and too many communities like them, have betrayed a greater trust and have more to apologize for than they have even begun to ponder. (*November 1991*)

WHILE WE'RE AT IT

■ Some significant progress has been made on "equal access" in public schools. That is to say, high schools that had allowed students to promote Marxist liberationism, gay rights, and goddess worship must now allow other students, if they are so inclined, to promote their Christian convictions. Americans United is, of course, on this case too. *Church & State* expresses support for a student who complains, "A group of students go around the school and approach you and say you're going to burn in hell. I feel it's wrong." Apparently it would be alright if they said that you're not going to burn in hell; even better if they said there is no hell; best yet if they didn't mention the subject. Now it's not nice being told that you're going to burn in hell, and no doubt a lot less nice to burn in hell. One response to people who have rather doleful views on your eternal destination is to tell them that you think they're wrong, and explain why. It is called, if we remember correctly, free speech. *(April 1992)*

■ We almost got away with it. But now Texe Marrs, who runs Living Truth Ministries in Austin, Texas, has told his thousands of readers the real story behind "Evangelicals and Catholics Together: The Christian Mission in the Third Millennium." It seems that Charles Colson is a "closet Catholic" who was recruited by the Vatican to arrange for Protestantism's surrender to Rome. Neuhaus is a "Marxist heretic" who answers to "both the notorious *Catholic Order of the Jesuits* and the infamous Christian-bashing, *Jewish Anti-Defamation League.*" "When Rev. Neuhaus abandoned the Lutheran Church to become a Catholic priest, the Vatican and its Jesuits knew they had a potential winner. With Rome's guidance (and financial means!), they reasoned, Richard Neuhaus could be used to manipulate millions of gullible Christians into joining in a grand crusade to destroy Protestantism." In light of Marrs' revelations, we can see how sneaky Neuhaus has been in covering his tracks by pretending on occasion to be critical of the Jesuits and the Anti-Defamation League. "Colson and Neuhaus openly admit that they secretly worked for two years behind the scenes on this project. Their plan was to get the world's top evangelical and Catholic leaders to sign up and endorse the manifesto before expected opposition developed." (In retrospect, it was probably a mistake for Chuck and me to admit it publicly.) Those who want to know more can get *All Fall Down*, a special report by Mr. Marrs that reveals "the stunning facts about the greatest sell-out in the history of Christianity." It seems that Protestants have been recruited to work with Jews and Jesuits to bring "the whole religious establishment, under their supreme leader, the Pope, straight into the Great Apostasy." In addition to the real dirt on Colson and Neuhaus, the report "unmasks the Vatican connections" of some of the biggest names in Protestantism, including Pat Robertson, Billy Graham, Bill Bright, Robert Schuller, Richard Land, and Larry Lewis. Oh yes, Marrs reveals that Neuhaus also publishes "a propagandistic magazine, *Things Considered*." Don't say you were not warned. (*February 1995*)

■ The wisdom of "coming out of the closet" is a sometimes thing. It depends on what one is coming out about. Consider this little item by Matthew Parris in the *Spectator* (London): "I was telephoned from Australia this week by a friend who for years has been struggling with the question of whether to conceal his homosexuality. I have always urged him not to, assuring him the best people respect honesty, modern society in Britain is tolerant of every human type, one should be true to oneself, etc. He recently came to the same conclusion and acted upon it, so far without ill-effect. But he had not telephoned about that. 'Matt,' he said, joyously, 'I've become a Christian. I'm born again. I went to this evangelist's meeting and the Lord Jesus came to me. I wanted to tell you immediately. I want to tell everybody. I want to shout 'Hallelujah!' All I could do was mumble, 'I'm pleased for you, Charlie.' Inwardly I thought, 'I hope he doesn't feel he has to tell everybody about it; it would be pretty embarrassing. At dinner

parties, I mean aren't some things best kept to oneself?' and, out loud to him, I caught myself saying, 'It's a big step to announce this sort of thing, Charlie. You'll lose friends. You ought to think twice and maybe keep it to yourself. . . .'"
(*January 1992*)

BOYS AND GIRLS:
THE LONG WAY BACK TO THE OBVIOUS

Surveys provide additional evidence that Americans are returning to "traditional values." Traditional values is usually a synonym for common sense or moral platitudes. Such sense is common and such morality is platitudinous because they are powerfully confirmed and reconfirmed by human experience over thousands of years. We now may be entering a new period of reconfirmation, notably in the realm of sexuality, and also among young people at college.

To be sure, college campuses sometimes look like the last holdout, increasingly turning themselves into enclaves of countercultural madnesses. It may be, however, that even some of the more bizarre developments on campus indicate that students, too, are returning to the morally obvious—although, to be sure, they are taking the very long way back. Consider, for example, the nationwide controversy over "date rape."

Here is a longish article in our most self-important local newspaper, reporting that students around the country are engaged in "a very public soul-searching unthinkable a generation ago. . . . Men and women are asking themselves and each other: When is sex considered sex, and when is sex considered rape?" The article is about very young men and very young women, otherwise known as boys and girls. And the question posed by the article is better understood as the difference between fornication (assumed to be OK) and rape (definitely bad). The current discussions about date rape that are lurching toward the self-evident were initiated, it is generally thought, by Susan Brownmiller's 1975 book, *Against Our Will: Men, Women, and Rape*. Ms. Brownmiller's polemic was hailed as yet another feminist broadside against "androcentric oppression" but, as we shall see, the debate that it sparked has thrown a number of feminist orthodoxies into severe question.

Date rape (also known as acquaintance rape) is when "sexual activity goes too far and becomes abhorrent to the woman." Some putative experts in "male studies" complain that that definition slights the situations in which sexual activity becomes abhorrent to the man, but, for very sensible reasons, that complaint is not being taken very seriously in the current discussion. The entire discussion of date rape is premised, with justice, upon an assumed inequality between male and female.

Jennifer Volchko of Lehigh University, an expert on date rape, says that "giving the problem a name has increased understanding and awareness of it." That makes sense. Presumably many boys, given the opportunity, have always tried to take sexual advantage of girls. One might speculate that the phenomenon has something to do with human nature, although, of course, talk about human nature is today banished from respectable academic discourse. What Ms. Volchko undoubtedly meant to say is that giving the phenomenon a "politically correct" name made it permissible to discuss it as a problem.

The thing under discussion has always had plenty of names: defilement, violation, debauchery, libertinism, wenching, and venery, for a few examples. None of those names would do, however, since they are associated with traditional moral discernments that are out of synch with contemporary orthodoxies about recreational sex. But now we have an ideologically acceptable name for the thing, date rape. This permits our experts to "discover" that boys in the heat of their libidinous prime frequently try to go as far as they can with girls. Science marches on.

A Readiness to Protest

Dr. Volchko explains that this generation of women was raised under the influence of the feminist movement and they are therefore more ready "to protest what is seen as men overstepping their bounds." But there is another part of that feminist movement that was set upon erasing the differences between men and women, especially with respect to sexual behavior. Women were determined to demonstrate that they were every bit as erotically aggressive and insatiable as men. That doctrine has been dropped in the debate over date rape.

In the present debate, we are back to traditional views of the male as rutting aggressor and the female as defender of decencies. Of course, more radical feminists have insisted for a long time that all heterosexual intercourse is equivalent to rape or prostitution. The college girls involved in the controversy at hand do not go that far. They appear prepared to "go along" with what boys so desperately want to do, but only after they have clearly given their permission. We are not quite back to the time when young women were advised to "Lie still and think of England," but maybe we're getting there.

At Brown University some coeds were so incensed about date rape that they went around writing on rest room walls (presumably women's rest rooms) the names of guilty boys. The fellows are not taking at all kindly to this. Some have protested that the women who now charge date rape did not say "no" at the time and did not physically resist. Others contend that the women encouraged their advances. According to the *Times*, "Women call that an after-the-fact excuse; sexual intercourse, they argue, should proceed from clear mutual consent." Preferably in writing, one gathers, and preferably at the beginning of the evening. Were that the practice, however, whatever else was scheduled for the evening (movie, rock concert, dinner, etc.) might seem like an insufferable postponement of what some young people would likely view as the main event.

The federal government has not neglected to finance research in this area. A study funded by the National Institute of Mental Health found that 7 percent of college girls "said they had experienced sexual assault in the previous twelve months." The admitted margin of error might make that 9 percent or 5 percent, but it is a lot of young women. The definition of "sexual assault" includes "intercourse by physical force, intercourse as a result of intentionally getting the woman intoxicated, or forcible oral or anal penetration." Terms such as "force" and "forcible" are subject to fine calibrations, it would seem, and presumably women are not to be held responsible for getting drunk. However shaky the findings, Americans will be glad to know that their tax dollars are at work in trying to figure out what boys will do in order to have sex with girls.

Equally gratifying is the fact that, according to this article, college administrators are also addressing the phenomenon. "One of the biggest reasons for date rape is the high level of consumption of alcohol on campus," we read. It is authoritatively reported that, when boys and girls are drunk, they are likely to do things that they would not do when sober. Another factor in date rape, it has been discovered, is "the introduction of dormitories shared by both sexes." One of the important things to know about this college generation, it seems, is that the proximity of nude or partially clothed members of the opposite sex in shared hallways, bathrooms, and bedrooms appears to increase the incidence and intensity of sexual arousal. Such arousal, in turn, frequently precipitates sexual suggestions and behavior. "Above all, assumptions about the roles of men and women seem to be shifting, with a resulting confusion on both sides about what is and is not acceptable behavior," the report continues. "It is clearly a perception issue," says Kim Gandy of the National Organization for Women, and it is hard to argue with that, whatever that means.

Remarkable Findings

In any event, federal and state funds are being made available for the establishment of "Sexual Assault Recovery Services" at universities across the country. At the same time, insurance companies are threatening to withdraw from the college market because of the rising incidence of claims related to date rape. Dr. Volchko thinks the rise of feminism has created a quite new situation. Date rape was not discussed in the old days, she says. "You didn't call it anything." The conventional thinking then, she said, was to say to the girl, "You put yourself in a vulnerable position and it's your own fault." Now, we are given to understand, it's the boy's fault.

The report continues, "College women, almost uniformly, complain about men assuming that certain behavior, like kissing or heavy petting, is an automatic precursor to intercourse. And they complain about the pervasiveness of these behavioral assumptions." In a family magazine such as this, we cannot detail what is meant by heavy petting, but we assume that a few readers, even those who are over thirty have some familiarity with the practice. The new research, however, has determined that, with a surprising degree of frequency, young men who are in the heat of heavy petting become quite urgent about wanting, as it is commonly put, "to go all the way."

These are among the remarkable findings of the studies of the current college generation, underscoring the truth that "assumptions about the roles of men and women seem to be shifting." There is yet another disturbing discovery: "Women interviewed on several campuses said that when they talk about sex in their dormitory rooms there is a high level of distrust of men." Women who went to college in an earlier time will no doubt regret the loss of innocence, remembering how they assumed that boys could be trusted not to be sexually importunate.

Public Confessions and Mixed Signals

At Lehigh University, the report continues, they have what appear to be Maoist-style "self-criticism sessions." For instance, one sexually active (as they say) young man claimed that he had never raped a woman. Under pressure, however, he admitted that he had had sex with a girl when they were both drunk and she had struggled initially. "But they all do," he added. "It's the way it works," he told the official in charge of the session. Finally he broke down and admitted that he was "very confused" and had in fact raped "some" of the girls he dated. "I was uninformed and incorrect in my actions," he wrote in his confession that was published in the Lehigh student newspaper. The *Times* report does not say, but we would like to assume that he was then forgiven his deviance from correct opinion.

University administrators said that the behavior of young men "is reinforced by pressure from other men to 'score.'" This novel turn is reinforced by other expectations. For instance, the experts say, "many men assume that when a woman enters their bedroom in a dorm or a fraternity house, it is an unspoken invitation to sex." It used to be, we are invited to believe, that when a girl came into a boy's bedroom both understood that she only wanted to have a heart-to-heart talk. But now, it seems, these boys always have sex on their minds. "College-age kids nowadays have a different attitude toward sex," says Lawrence K. Pettit, chancellor of Southern Illinois University.

Girls and boys are missing signals. "At certain fraternity houses, when the girl goes upstairs, the guys start licking their chops," says Brett Finn, a junior at Lehigh. "There is a real miscommunication." At Lehigh, it seems, it used to be understood that girls go upstairs in fraternity houses for other reasons, like making sure the boys cleaned up their bedrooms.

Chancellor Pettit adds, "The kids regard sex almost as an entitlement, certainly as an expectation." But why shouldn't they? one might ask. They have repeatedly been told, not least in the schools, that regular genital exercise is a natural requisite of mental and psychic health. In these enlightened times it is understood that sex is recreational—good clean fun, demystified of the moral inhibitions of the past. The old notion that sex has consequences has been nullified by the pill and by abortion-as-contraception. In the new context, a girl's refusal to join in a refreshing little workout must seem irrational and downright unfriendly.

Date rape research has turned up other dynamics at work. For instance: "Many men have been conditioned to believe that initial refusals are an essential part of a 'mating game' ritual, one that dictates that women must resist somewhat to make themselves more attractive to men." Note that the boys have allegedly been "conditioned" to believe in mating rituals. Perhaps what is missing in the background of some journalists and sex researchers is, quite literally, a measure of familiarity with the birds and the bees. A person has to be conditioned *not* to understand that human beings, like all God's creatures, are programmed to engage in mating rituals involving male aggression and female submission. However, human beings, unlike other creatures, are not determined to follow the program. Over the millennia they have developed mores, taboos, and protective institutions aimed at inhibiting the male from doing what comes naturally.

Rape Unlimited

Rape is a mortal sin and odious crime. One of the unhappier aspects of the controversy over date rape is that, under ideological pressures, rape is trivialized. Rape, as currently discussed, does not have to involve physical assault in any way. Cornell's Andrea Parrot, who has pushed the idea that there is a date rape epidemic, claims that "any sexual intercourse without mutual desire is a form of rape." An article in *New York* magazine explains the logic: "In other words, a woman is being raped if she has sex when not in the mood, even if she fails to inform her partner of that fact." An expert in Columbia University's date-rape-education program declares, "Every time you have an act of intercourse, there must be explicit consent, and if there's no explicit consent, then it's rape. Stone silence throughout an entire physical encounter with someone is not explicit consent."

A training manual at Swarthmore College goes further: "acquaintance rape spans a spectrum of incidents and behaviors ranging from crimes legally defined as rape to verbal harassment and inappropriate innuendo." Little wonder, therefore, that Catherine Nye, a psychologist at the University of Chicago, found that 43 percent of the women in a widely cited rape study "had not realized they had been raped." Radical feminists insist that any sexual experience that involves confusion or ambivalence constitutes rape. If that is true, surely 100 percent of women who have had sexual intercourse have been raped, for it is difficult to imagine anyone "doing it," at least the first time, without a measure of confusion or ambivalence. Such bizarre reasoning can only result in voiding the horror of what sensible people mean by rape.

No Reason for Saying No

Nonetheless, the date rape debate can be welcomed in other respects. For all the ludicrous social scientific jargon in which it is wrapped, it is an instance of confused groping toward the reinvention of the wheel. Most welcome is the acknowledgment of fundamental and incorrigible differences between men and women when it comes to sexual behavior. In negotiating the shoals of erotic passion and practice, women are at a distinct disadvantage—obviously in physical strength but also in controlling the dynamics of the sexual encounter. Every culture known to us has recognized this reality and has therefore nurtured habits, expectations, and institutions designed to defend the woman against male aggressiveness. The odd thing about our cultural moment is that the women who so enthusiastically liberated themselves from those defenses now complain that they are defenseless.

One need only add that the biblically supported patterns of defense and restraint center in chastity, marriage, and respect for persons. It is said that these traditional ways of dealing with sexual behavior are "unrealistic" when so many young people think they are entitled to regular sex. That is much like saying that driving sober is unrealistic when so many young people think it is alright to drive drunk. Putting the focus on chastity, marriage, and self-restraint will not solve the "problem" of youthful sexuality. Nothing will do that. There will be, as there always have been, frequent deviations from approved behavior. For that there is social censure and, for the repentant, forgiveness. But there is surely nothing more unrealistic than the notion that autonomous, liberated boys and girls at the height of libidinous commotions are going to invent for themselves, starting from square one and maybe in a dormitory bedroom, a new sexual ethic.

The date rape debate is a poignant cry for the reestablishment of the idea of moral limits that many, notably feminists, recklessly abandoned in the name of self-actualization. At the end of the *Times* article, one of the experts quoted manages, once again, to get everything entirely backward. He is describing the rape education programs now being initiated in freshmen orientation sessions. The freshmen are told, he says, "Don't expect sex on every date. Ask a woman what she feels comfortable doing or not doing." It is embarrassing to have to instruct instructors on the simple fact that, so long as many young men think sex might be an option that night, they are going to do their darndest to get it. And to ask a girl what she is comfortable with at six o'clock may have little to do with twelve o'clock. Too many young men think it is their role to push the comfort level as far as they can, and then some.

Most important, the expert in question misses the point that his "education" puts the entire burden on the young woman to draw the line. What women are demanding in the debate over date rape is that some lines be drawn that are binding on everybody—lines that are defined not in terms of "comfort" but of right and wrong. Unless a young woman can say no because it is morally wrong, she has—in the moment of sexual encounter with a companion of her own choosing—no very convincing reason for saying no at all. It is little wonder that, over the last twenty years or so, many men were very supportive of women who practiced unilateral moral disarmament in the name of liberation. The date rape debate, although coming too late for many women, was inevitable. It is, whether those involved realize it or not, a return to basics in one of the most basic spheres of human behavior. But, oh, what a long, long way we are taking to get back to the obvious. (*May 1991*)

GETTING TOUGH ON CRIME IN WISCONSIN

"Apartment for rent. 1 bedroom, electric included, mature Christian handyman." Beverly Schnell put that ad in the *Hartford Times Press* in December 1990. She now owes Wisconsin's Civil Rights Bureau $8,000, having been found guilty of discriminating on the basis of sex ("handyman") and religion ("Christian"). One wonders why "mature" did not get her charged with ageism. The Bureau has made it clear that she would be just as guilty if her for-rent ad had been placed in a church bulletin or a grocery store bulletin board. "I had put a general ad in the paper and got all kinds of weirdos," said Ms. Schnell. "I got harassed by all kinds of people because of that ad. I live alone, and I needed some security and someone to help me with the house. I had no idea and no intention of discriminating against anybody. The terms 'Christian' and 'handyman' are common terms that I thought everybody uses." Not anymore they can't.

Apparently, Ms. Schnell used "Christian" to indicate reliable and upright in character. It is perhaps a nice compliment to Christians, but such compliments can be costly. If Ms. Schnell seriously meant that she would only rent to a professing and practicing Christian, she might be in really big trouble. As it is, she may only have to sell her house in order to pay the $8,000 penalty. LeAnna Ware, director of the Civil Rights Bureau, said, "Under the law, you don't have a right to discriminate, so in effect you can't put anyone you want in your house." Put differently, you can't keep anyone you don't want out of your house. Civil rights means that you have lost control of your house. Civil rights has been turned to mean so many things, so why not this?

There is also an interesting subject/object distinction engaged here. Let's say the subject is the person placing the ad, and the object the person responding. Can the subject be discriminating in how she describes herself? "Christian homeowner desiring security on premises and person with fix-it skills offers apartment for rent, 1 bedroom, electric included." That leaves it for the respondent to infer that she's looking for a Christian handyman. It is not clear whether the Civil Rights Bureau's sleuths combing the classifieds would let that pass. The proposed ad describes the subject rather than the object of the search. Can it be a crime to describe oneself as one wishes? "Jewish philanthropic organization looking for an executive director." One might reasonably infer they want a Jew. Perhaps that, too, is criminal in Wisconsin. The end result of this curious idea of discrimination is the criminalizing not of what you do to others but of what you are.

In fact, a lawyer friend points out, the classifieds are loaded with blatant discriminations. This is especially true of the "personals" in papers such as the *Village Voice* and somewhat classier publications such as the *New York Review of Books*. Trips, jobs, living space, companionship, and much else is tendered to those who meet explicitly stated criteria ranging from race, religion (or non-religion), and musical tastes to sadomasochistic proclivities. We expect that such classifieds are published even in Wisconsin. Ms. Ware's Bureau would seem to have plenty of work on its hands. "Gay homeowner offers apartment for rent, 1 bedroom, electric included. Fun-loving handyman." For some reason we doubt that that ad would trigger the attentions of the civil rights police.

We only regret that Ms. Schnell did not really intend to discriminate, that she did not as a matter of religious conviction insist upon a Christian handyman (all right, handyperson). If she had, we might have had an interesting test of the Religious Freedom Restoration Act just passed by Congress. In that event, Ms. Ware's office would have had to demonstrate a "compelling state interest" that prevents Beverly Schnell from having a Christian handyman in her house. Given the zealotry of the antidiscrimination constabulary, we do not doubt that Ms. Ware might have tried. Given the ease with which the slightest state interest is deemed to be compelling in overriding religious freedom, we do not doubt that she might have won. Then, instead of just facing the prospect of having to sell her house, Ms. Schnell might be facing truly

onerous penalties. Perhaps Wisconsin has jail terms for mid-
dle-aged ladies who want a Christian handyman on the
premises. Whom the gods would destroy . . . (*March 1994*)

HOW TO HANDLE TOUGH QUESTIONS

Parishes of the Evangelical Lutheran Church in America
(ELCA) are debating a fifty-five-page draft study of sexuality
and Christian faith. A final draft is supposed to be ready for
the 1993 national assembly of the 5.2 million member body.
Bishop Herbert Chilstrom, executive head of the ELCA, is
among those worried that the church may be headed for a
wrenchingly divisive battle, similar to the conflicts that have
wracked Presbyterians and Methodists, especially over the
question of homosexuality. In a recent interview he suggested
that it might be better to let the church deal with sexuality in
its own time and in its own way, without the necessity of voting things up or down. "That is exactly what happened with
the issue of divorce," Chilstrom said. "In the field of divorce,
a sea of change has taken place. We have bishops who are
divorced. That would have been unheard of ten years ago.
We've become realistic, acknowledging that there are some
marriages that should not continue." He suggests that, in time,
the church might become equally realistic about homosexuality, refusing to judge the question "by aberrations among
homosexuals." Homophobia, we are given to understand, gets
in the way of calm deliberation.

The bishop has a point. Among Lutherans, as with other
oldline churches, it was not long ago that divorce was cause for
removal from the church's ministry. Today the divorce rate
among clergy in such churches is about the same as in the general population. It is not that unusual for pastors and seminary
professors to be divorced several times, in some instances having swapped spouses. So what's the big deal about divorce?

Many people have difficulty remembering that not long ago these churches spoke with apparent seriousness about the indissolubility of marriage as a sacred bond. "What God has joined together," and all that. As the bishop says, no decision was made to change the church's teaching on marriage and divorce. It just happened.

And so ten years from now out-of-the-closet homosexuals will be ordained to the ministry and it will all seem quite natural. What was the big deal about homosexuality? folks will ask. The trick, as Bishop Chilstrom suggests, is to avoid forcing people to make decisions about what is true and false, what is right and wrong, and other institutionally disruptive questions. In sum, go with the flow. Unless churches learn to transcend the outdated dichotomies of true/false and right/wrong, they will never know the institutional peace that can only be securely grounded in theological and moral indifference. As the bishop says, "a sea of change" is underway. (*August/September 1992*)

FT

THE COMING AGE OF RELIGION

La Revanche de Dieu was the French title and it caused something of a stir there. Here the book by Gilles Kepel is called *The Revenge of God: The Resurgence of Islam, Christianity, and Judaism in the Modern World* (Pennsylvania State University Press, $35). We were struck by this comment in the *Economist*: "In the contentious admixture of politics and religion, Mr. Kepel is most unusual in not seeking to press a particular view, still less to win converts for any religion or none. . . . And he is persuasive when he concludes that, for better and worse, the political influence of religion will be much greater than it has been in the recent past, not least because today's religious activists are better educated, better off, and more articulate than yesterday's." It is but one of many such comments in recent years, often from unlikely sources and usually expressed in uneasy tones. The assumed link between modernity and secularization did not hold. History is not turning out the way we were educated to think it would. Religion is back, and in a very big way.

There is something to what the *Economist* says about the educational factor, no doubt. On the world scene there are today more well-educated and articulate Muslims than was the case, say, forty years ago. Well-educated and articulate, that is, in Western terms, which enables them to more confidently challenge the hegemony of secular liberal ideas generated by the West. Here in the U.S., the *Economist's* generalization would apply to Evangelical Protestants and Roman Catholics, both of whom were more marginal—some say ghettoized—forty years ago. On the other hand, there were hosts of well-educated, well-off, and articulate religious activists of oldline Protestantism in the past. If religion did not seem to be politically influential (i.e., politically intrusive) then, it is likely because oldline activism was basically in sync with what secular liberalism defined as progress. The civil rights movement that segued into the anti-Vietnam War movement and then into sundry movements of what used to be called the counterculture is the outstanding case in point.

In the current culture wars over everything from abortion to homosexual rights and parental choice in education, however, religious activism is typically contrary to the elite liberal idea of progress. Therefore it is perceived that "the political influence of religion is greater." Religion in this context means culturally conservative religion. Liberal religious activism is by no means dead, although its institutional base has been weakened by the continuing decline of the oldline churches. But such activism is not very visible; it is not likely to occasion comments about the growing influence of religion in public life. In oldline Protestantism, the demise of *Christianity and Crisis* last year was a significant sign. The *Christian Century* picked up its shrunken subscription list, but seems disinclined to pick up its banner of more or less uncritical leftism. Among Catholics, the *National Catholic Reporter* appears to do well, being packed with advertisements for courses and institutes pressing sixtiesh agendas that otherwise show up nowhere on the American political screen. The audience may be ageing, but the *NCR* academic and catechetical networks are constant. Others may want to debate whether that is a case of keeping the faith or being stuck in a time warp.

On the Left

Outside the churches in which it is based, religious activism on the left does not get much attention these days for a number of reasons. One reason is that the advocacy of the oldline church-and-society curia (among, for example, Presbyterians USA, United Methodists, Episcopalians, and ELCA Lutherans) is not readily distinguishable from the positions advanced by, say, the editorial board of the *New York Times* or from the conventional wisdom in the faculty lounges of the nation's colleges and universities. In such elite centers of opinion and influence, what the oldline churches have to say is neither threatening nor very interesting. That was not always the case. Thirty and more years ago—with respect to civil rights, Vietnam, and various social agitations—religious activism was seen to play an important part in providing moral legitimation for movements of change. One thinks of groups such as the Fellowship of Reconciliation and Clergy and Laity Concerned About Vietnam, and about individuals such as the Berrigan brothers, William Sloane Coffin, and, in a category by himself, Martin Luther King, Jr. For anyone under forty, these are all names from the olden days.

It might be argued that one reason the religious left seems inconsequential, even nonexistent, is that the secular left no longer needs it. What in the 1960s was called "the long march through the institutions" has now been accomplished, and yesterday's revolutionaries have become, without changing their minds about much of importance, today's establishment. This new "correlation of forces" (as the Marxists used to say) should not be exaggerated. The long march has largely triumphed in the media, the universities, the big foundations, the liberal churches, and much of the business elite. Those are impressive conquests, to be sure, but even in those worlds the conquest is not total. And those worlds do not control our political culture, as is evident in the continuing ascendancy of conservatism in our public life. To speak of such an ascendancy assumes, of course, that the presidential election of 1992 was a fluke in which the winning candidate, although presenting himself as a conservative Democrat, received fewer votes than Michael Dukakis in 1988, and now appears to be anything but ascendant.

But back to religious activism and why we hear incessantly about the religious right but almost never about the religious left. In most political and cultural analyses, the religious left does not figure because it is no longer important to the establishmentarian left; it is superfluous. There is no felt need for its moral legitimation, if indeed it is capable of providing such. Thirty years ago, the editorial pages of the prestige media referred respectfully to pronouncements by, for example, the National Council of Churches. That simply does not happen today. Many editorialists are probably not aware that there is something called the National Council of Churches. As Stanley Rothman and others have suggested, that may be because of a growing indifference to religion among media elites. But one notes that the same elites are keenly aware of, hysterically aware of, the religious right. The religious left is still very much there, but it does not threaten and it does not offer anything that the culture elites view as substantively or strategically valuable. There are one or two exceptions. The homosexual movement, which is now securely ensconced in large sectors of the elite, does seek moral legitimation from the religious left in the form of ordaining active gays and blessing same-sex unions. And some liberal churches still provide moral cover for the unlimited abortion license. Other exceptions do not come readily to mind.

In his insightful study *Representing God*, sociologist Allen Hertzke analyzes the ways in which churches of all varieties can be effective "mediating institutions" by giving their members a voice in the American polity, and also by interpreting public debates to their own constituencies. But on the most critical issue in our culture wars, namely abortion, there is an important disparity between left and right. Hertzke notes that conservative religious lobbies generally take a stronger pro-life position than their constituencies, while liberal lobbies are more strongly pro-choice than their supporters. The important disparity is this: conservative denominations represent their most active and most committed members in taking a strong pro-life position; liberal denominations, taking a strong pro-choice position, are representing the view of their least active and least committed members. American Baptists are pro-choice and Southern Baptists are pro-life, but an active American Baptist is more likely to be pro-life than a less active Southern Baptist. The same pattern holds for Catholics, Episcopalians, Pentecostals, Lutherans, and apparently everybody else. The crucial factor is *participation*; the more a church member is active and committed, the more likely that person will be pro-life. And the divide over abortion is far and away the most important defining line with respect to other agitated questions in our public life.

What is perceived as the growing influence of religion in our public life is probably real enough. But the perception is heightened by the fact that the religion getting attention is the religion that challenges the status quo, namely, the "religious right." Conservatives will continue to complain, and understandably so, that it is unfair for the media to keep on talking about the religious right while almost never mentioning the religious left. But the unfairness, if unfairness it be, will likely continue. For the reasons discussed above, in the view of those who shape the media story lines the religious left does not matter. It makes little or no substantive contribution in terms of ideas or moral legitimacy; and it has long since been evident that its constituency is typically the least committed of the churches most in decline. To paraphrase Stalin: How many divisions does the religious left have? Unlike Stalin's colossal misjudgment of the pope, that seems a reasonable question.

One might ask whether we have not reached a sorry state when religion is discussed in terms of divisions for fighting political and cultural wars. That is an excellent question, and the answer is that we have reached the sorry state when such discussion is inescapable. Robert Wuthnow of Princeton has carefully examined the ways in which the major church bodies are riddled through and through with the polarized politics of our society. The politicizing of religion and the religionizing of politics go hand in hand. One can understand the complaint that it was the liberals who started it: back in the 1960s, back in the modernist-fundamentalist controversies of the 1920s, back in the social gospel movement of the late nineteenth century. Now, the conservatives say, the religious left is discovering that two can play at the game of politics. And there does seem to be a kind of rough justice in that way of looking at matters. Rough justice and great danger.

Keeping Politics in its Place

Because politics is a function of culture and at the heart of culture is morality and at the heart of morality is religion, there is a necessary and unavoidable interaction between politics and religion. But the conflation of politics and religion is the death of authentic politics and the death of authentic religion. In the Christian account of things, politics deals with the penultimate, with proximate justice in a fallen world where we await the right ordering of all things in the genuinely new politics of the Kingdom Come. Faith attends to transcendent truth that encompasses and informs our earthly tasks, including politics, but can never be taken captive to such tasks. The conflation of politics and religion that results in religionized politics cannot help but seem threatening, not only to secularists but to Christians and Jews who understand the modesty and fragility of the political project. It cannot help but appear as "La Revanche de Dieu," a sword of vengeance wielded by those who presume to act as punishing angels of the Lord.

We have little doubt that the political influence of religion will come in for increasing attention in the years ahead. Alternative plausibility structures (as Peter Berger calls them) have collapsed or are collapsing. The comatose state of secular liberal theory will not likely be reversed by the desperate efforts of John Rawls, Ronald Dworkin, and their like. Secularists such as Richard Rorty and his friends have long been doing their ironic jig on liberalism's grave. And outside academic covens of impenetrable nostalgia, the quasi-religious worldview of Marxist socialism, once so uncritically embraced, is being forgotten with embarrassed haste. New ideologies will emerge, no doubt. As Orwell observed, there seems to be almost no limit to what intellectuals can invent to believe. But for the foreseeable future it seems to be the case, as it has not been the case for more than two hundred years, that the only plausibility structures left standing are religious. More precisely, religion—notably the Abrahamic faiths: Judaism, Christianity, and Islam—offer the only comprehensive belief systems that command the allegiance of hundreds of millions of people and propose, however confusedly, a direction toward the right ordering of the world.

This is not an unqualifiedly good thing, nor is it to say that religion is unchallenged. The challenges are legion and have many names: unfaith, bad faith, hedonism, hubris, and nihilism. In addition, a credible case can be made that technology and science have become quasi-religious belief systems that will, as Jacques Ellul and others have warned, undo the human project—and that sooner rather than later. And of course the ascendancy of religion is not an unqualifiedly good thing because religion, as a human enterprise, is as riddled with corruption and potential for evil as any other enterprise of sinful humanity. In some ways the dangers are greater with religion. Religion's invocation of absolute authority can excite fanaticism, and can exclude critical challenges just as rigorously as religion itself has frequently been excluded from public discourse in the modern era.

Although there is no way of avoiding that danger altogether, three observations are in order. First, the capacity for ideological craziness seems to be a permanent feature of the human condition. Second, the primary instances in the modern world of such craziness turning murderously mad have been fanatically antireligious in character, from the Great Terror of the French Revolution to Marxism-Leninism and

Nazism in this century. Third, when religion degenerates into ideology—becoming a set of ideas in the service of political power—the resources for correction are found within religion itself. This is notably true of the prophetically self-critical tradition of the Bible and, in the Christian rendering of reality, of the cross as the definitive judgment upon earthly pretensions to power.

Cause of Freedom, Claims of Truth

So where does this leave us with respect to the widespread and growing anxiety about the political influence of religion? We cannot tell the anxious that there is nothing to worry about. There is a great deal to worry about in terms of the debasement of both religion and politics. Not only can we agree with the anxious that there is much to be anxious about, but we must caution enthusiastic religionists that their ascendancy cannot be unambiguously equated with the will of God and the advancement of the common good. At the same time, it is surely cause for thanksgiving that the great spasms of militant secularism seem to be exhausting themselves, at least for now. The third millennium portends a continuing resurgence of religion's public potency, especially in the case of Islam and Christianity. On the world scene, Islam is not monolithic. The trick is to nurture and encourage those Muslim developments that are compatible with and can even strengthen the achievements of democratic pluralism, achievements that owe a great debt to liberalism.

Elsewhere, the public resurgence of religion marks a new chapter in a very long Christian story of trying to figure out the right relationship between Church and culture, Christ and Caesar, the city of God and the city of man. There is no reason to assume that this or the next generation is going to get that relationship any more nearly correct than did the Christians at the time of Theodosius, Charlemagne, or Jonathan Edwards. When Jesus said His followers were to be in but not of the world He was proposing a conundrum that awaits eschatological resolution. Meanwhile, we have no choice but to work at getting it right, or at least at getting it less wrong than we often have in the past. Among Christians, it seems that the larger part of that work will have to be done by Catholics and evangelical Protestants. This is a reality boldly faced by the declaration "Evangelicals and Catholics Together," published in FIRST THINGS, May 1994.

In this country, the pattern of "convergence and coopera- tion" affirmed in that declaration will continue to be referred to by some, with fear and loathing, as "the religious right." One hopes that more will come to recognize that the political reengagement of religiously inspired citizens and their call to greater moral reflectiveness about how we ought to live together is a sign of the rejuvenation of a democratic experi- ment returned to its founding presuppositions. "We hold these truths" was the beginning of the conversation that launched this experiment, and it should now be obvious to all that the experiment cannot be sustained by a secular liberalism that divorced the cause of freedom from the claims of truth. Those who now fear publicly resurgent religion will in time, one hopes, come to recognize that freedom grounded in moral truth provides a greater security for virtues cherished by old- fashioned liberals—openness, rationality, tolerance, and mutual respect. But that may take a long time.

Meanwhile, the culture war will be prosecuted, whether we like it or not. And the question of abortion—the question of who belongs to the community that is protected in law and life—will continue to be at the center of the many battles of the culture war. The more strident defenders of the status quo will continue to rail against the "religious right," and invoke the "separation of church and state," by which they mean the separation of religion and religiously based moral judgment from public life. One can predict with absolute certainty that there will continue to be excesses by religious activists that will warrant the most robust railing. But all things considered, the continuing resurgence of publicly potent religion seems all but inevitable. As aforesaid, that is not unqualifiedly good news; and we are well reminded that history is notorious for playing surprises both cruel and benign. If the culture war and the political influence of religion work out along the lines here suggested, however, one hopes that those who welcome and those who fear this development will come to recognize it not as the revenge but as the mercy of God. *(June/July 1994)*

FT

AGAINST PEER FEAR

One regularly gets inquiries from aspiring writers eager to be published. So it always has been, and so it should be. Quite possibly, there is right now some aspiring twenty-five-year-old graduate student working on her first major article that we will be pleased to feature in a forthcoming issue. Although we publish only a very small portion of all the manuscripts received, a significant portion of what we do publish arrives unsolicited (over the transom, as they say). Frequently an author will say in his covering letter that, while the present piece may not be ready for prime time, he would appreciate editorial criticism of his efforts. The press of duties tends to make such detailed criticism impossible, but a word or two of general advice might be helpful. As will be seen, the following word is about more than getting published.

Perhaps nothing so prevents good articles from being written, or so spoils good articles that are written, than what we might call peer fear. Of course we are talking chiefly about academic authors (and most of our authors are academics in one way or another). Peer fear results in not writing for a general audience, not even writing to make a clear argument, but, rather, looking over one's shoulder at what colleagues in "the guild" might think. The product, all too often, is not an article but a kind of sprawling annotated bibliography—"as X says, although taking into account Y's emendation as elaborated by P," and so forth. Annotated bibliographies are useful things, as are florilegiums of pertinent opinions on a given subject, but they are not articles.

The trick is to find what is sometimes called one's own voice.

Here is the subject, here is why it is important, and this is what I have to say about it that nobody else seems to have said, or at least not to have said in quite this way. What Richard Roarbee and Catherine McUpures and Jacques Dadildo have said on the subject may be very interesting—and, at least obliquely, the author should ordinarily evidence a familiarity with the arguments made by such worthies—but in this office we work on the assumption that people read an article because they hope that *this* author has something important to say to them.

Academic Thought Control

To be sure, it is easy for us to deplore the toll exacted by peer fear, but pity the poor graduate students and junior faculty who have good reason to fear their peers if they are ever to obtain job security and the grand prize of tenure. It is no accident, as our Marxist friends used to say, that many, if not most, of our featured authors are either safely tenured or comfortably removed from the cramped arenas of academic combat. Although it is a source of constant wonder how many of the securely tenured are still intimidated by peer fear. They will privately grumble about the "smelly little orthodoxies" that hold so much of academe in thrall, but they are not about to make themselves difficult. Others among senior faculty are preoccupied with their academic specialities which is fair enough, and yet others take tenure to mean retirement from serious work, which is not fair at all but is part of a system that very few people have a vested interest in challenging.

For academics of both the ensconced and imperiled variety, writing for a journal such as this is usually not a smart career move. The ensconced need not worry, but the junior aspirant has no choice but to worry about what will look good on his resume when his name comes up before the tenure committee at Toetheline U. Items written for and within "the discipline" will receive a sympathetic nod, while it is deemed suspiciously unprofessional to have written for a "general audience," never mind in a journal well known to be annoyingly incorrect. The place to publish is in "scholarly" journals sponsored by the relevant academic guild, and in such journals prospective articles are "refereed" by a company of one's peers.

We don't know about structural engineering and brain surgery, but in the fields more pertinent to our interests—e.g., theology, philosophy, ethics, legal theory, cultural criticism— refereeing is, increasingly, censorship with respect not to competence but to orthodoxy. We have no objection to censorship in principle—after all, editors are inescapably in the censorship business, whether they like to admit it or not—but we do object to material that gives evidence of having been written in sweated anxiety not to push the buttons of angry ideologues who presume to guard what is published "in the field." When it comes to deciding whether to run an article or, for that matter, whether to give it a serious reading, a reliable rule of thumb is to exclude anything that looks like it might have been refereed. There are those scholarly journals for that kind of thing, even if nobody reads them.

That may sound anti-intellectual, but in reality there is nothing more anti-intellectual than the party lines that today dominate so much of academic writing and discourse. Sometimes it is Marxist (yes, Virginia, there are still Marxists), sometimes racialist (advanced in the cause of combatting racism), sometimes feminist (and, if radical, likely lesbian), and, increasingly, sometimes gay. Of course fine scholarship is still being done in many places, and of course specialized journals are necessary for specialized purposes, and, yes, we confess to reading with more than cursory attention the scholarly publications that we must.

But one gets the impression that most academics (at least those who have not confused tenure with retirement) have turned themselves round and round, burrowing ever deeper into the holes of "their" questions, while others eagerly feed their anger on pet resentments such as those marked out by the ideological lines mentioned above. Such is the corruption of the intellectual life in our time, or—and one notes this with relief—the limited part of the intellectual life that is dependent upon the university. Such is the unhappy circumstance of those academics caught in the paralyzing grip of peer fear.

Who Is "Qualified"?

Here at hand is a letter from yet another young professor, this one in a Methodist seminary. Did we know that at his school it has been baldly stated that nobody will get tenure who does not enhance the faculty's "inclusiveness"—meaning nobody who is not female, a person of color, or assertively homosexual? Well, no, we didn't know it about that school, but why should it be different? A distinguished theologian at a prestige university tells us that he advises his white, male doctoral students to have some more practicable backstop if they're thinking of an academic career. At a once distinguished nondenominational seminary, a young black woman was recently appointed associate professor, with tenure. She had not quite completed her doctoral thesis, but the appointments committee was assured that it would be ever so creative.

Raising questions about "qualifications" elicits a knowing sneer from the ideologically perfected. To *be* a woman, or a gay, or a person of color, or a member of any group certifiably marginal is itself qualification more than enough. To those who protest the unfairness and dishonesty of the system, the answer is that now outsiders are getting the advantage of unfair preferences that used to be enjoyed only by insiders. In speaking this way, people apparently do not recognize that they are casting contempt upon the disciplines and institutions of which they are part. It is and always has been a power game, they say, and the spoils go to those who play the game without scruple. Fancy talk about excellence and academic achievement simply disguises the nature of the game. Anyway—and with maximum offense to the racists, sexists, and homophobes who don't like it—we who once claimed to be fighting The System are now in charge of it. And that's the way things are.

A reader might object that this picture of the academy—notably in theology, philosophy, and associated fields—is altogether too bleak. We take no joy in bearing bad news, but the reader is wrong. Admittedly, the lines of fear are drawn differently at some Evangelical Protestant and Catholic institutions. Rather than race, gender, and sexual orientation, the Evangelical lines may be drawn at the question of biblical inerrancy or, at other schools, one may be excluded for having a favorable word to say about those awful fundamentalists. While Catholic scholars who suggest, for example, that this pontificate may actually have something to teach of theological worth definitely do not have a brilliant career in prospect. They will not be invited to the right (meaning, usually, left) academic conferences, nor will their papers pass peer review. And if they write intellectually serious books, they will likely be published by alternative presses, although a few might sneak their way on to the lists of publishers of academic respectability. (Among Catholics, alternative presses include Ignatius, which publishes supposed antiques such as de Lubac, von Balthasar, and Karol Wojtyla, a.k.a. John Paul II.)

Cowardice and Conformity

The contemporary academy is, to put it delicately, deeply corrupted by cowardice and conformity, which are mutually reinforcing. This is not to imply that those who dissent from the ideologically correct are consistently possessed of intelligence and talent unjustly spurned. That company has more than its fair share of cranks, and of mediocrities in search of any excuse for being such. But the onus rests on those responsible for the sorry state of higher education. On presidents who chiefly preside over endowments, deans who buy peace at any price, junior faculty who go along to get along, and senior faculty who stopped going anywhere a long time ago.

It is wrongheaded to blame the militant ideologues who are, after all, only doing what they say they are doing, conducting the long march through the institutions, a march that has resulted in triumphs with no end in sight. Having exacted agreement on the dangerously simplified proposition that there is no such thing as objective, value-free search for truth, they are making the most of the license to be outrageously and enragedly partisan in their declared war against civility, fairness, and disinterested inquiry. The consequence is that the academy today is, in very large part, the enemy of the intellectual life.

152

Of all the actors mentioned, only the junior faculty and graduate students warrant a measure of sympathy. What are they to do when their positions, their futures, their very livelihoods depend upon the ideological passions of petty tyrants? True, they could leave the academy to make an honest living, but some of them believe that they have something like a vocation, and maybe they do. Perhaps the present pestilence is designed to test vocations. The almost inescapable peer fear may lead to trimming at the edges, but the occasional accommodation of cowardice need not be craven. Most people are not cut out to be heroes, and it is understandable that they do not want to be thought difficult. In a highly disagreeable world, there is a good deal to be said for being likeable and liked. As Norfolk proposed to Sir Thomas in Robert Bolt's play *A Man for All Seasons*, why not go along for friendship's sake? Thus is cowardice confused with congeniality.

Needed: Resisters

What these young people desperately need is exemplars of resistance, maybe even of courage, within the academy. Their elders who resist will typically be in safe positions, thus diminishing somewhat the glitter of their courage, but they could at some point, in some institutions, form a critical mass that assures their juniors that there just might be life after the defiance of peer fear. Toward that end, we publish a journal, conduct conferences, and sponsor research projects that aim to nurture the intellectual life. It sounds embarrassingly old-fashioned, but we are devoted to inquiry that is intelligent and free, and to an inclusiveness that includes different and sometimes conflicting convictions. That devotion puts this journal and similar enterprises (for there are, thank God, others) in an awkward and sometimes painful relationship to the contemporary academy.

Many years ago, this writer was in a seminar with the late Saul Alinsky, the radical community organizer who founded the Industrial Areas Foundation. "Decide right now," said Alinsky to the gathered seminarians, "whether you want to be a bishop." His point was that those with episcopal ambitions were wasting their time in his course. And so we say, somewhat more gently, to the aspiring young academic who is interested in publishing here: Give careful thought to whether you can live with the prospect of not getting tenure. All the counter-pressures notwithstanding, there are an encouraging number of young scholars who seem prepared to live with that prospect, or at least to risk it. Those who have arrived on the far side of peer fear are, one is inclined to think, more likely to do something worthwhile with the tenure that, despite all, they may one day attain. *(May 1993)*

FT

WHILE WE'RE AT IT

■ Some years ago, Monsignor Harry Byrne of Epiphany Church in Manhattan visited The Hermitage in St. Petersburg. Commenting on Leonardo da Vinci's painting of the Virgin and Child, the young guide mentioned some technical details and then said, "The subject of this painting is 'Maternity.'" So effectively had her Marxist training erased any awareness of Mary and Our Lord, or so aware was she of what it was not permitted to say in public. The incident came to mind when a priest in upstate New York asked Msgr. Byrne what to do about a village atheist who was suing to have a creche removed from a public space. Byrne, who is no slouch on church-state relations, told the priest about the legal niceties and then offered a suggestion. "It's a long shot, but you might take away the halos, rearrange the angels, remove any words proclaiming divinity, and then caption the display, 'Maternity.' Everyone could then interpret the display as they wish." It worked under Communist oppression. Maybe we could get away with it under the oppression of currently cocka-mamie court rulings on religion in public. *(December 1991)*

■ Some readers may not believe it, but we really do not comment on every fatuity championed by the likes of the American Civil Liberties Union. There simply is not space. Here, for instance, is an item we never got around to. Local judges in Milwaukee have abandoned the long-standing practice of not evicting tenants from their homes during Christmas week. Landlords have always protested the practice, and now they have the support of the ACLU. "The moratorium serves no legal purpose and has the effect of promoting the religious celebration of Christmas," Gretchen Miller of the ACLU told the courts. "No similar rules prevent eviction of Muslim tenants during the month of Ramadan or the eviction of Jewish tenants during Passover, Rosh Hashanah, or other commonly celebrated religious holidays." Never mind that less than one-quarter of one percent of the population of Milwaukee is Muslim, and a Jew has not been evicted within living memory. Never mind that the courts are quite prepared to extend the practice to Muslims and Jews as the occasion arises. In a democracy, as defined by the ACLU, social reality must not be permitted to impinge upon the administration of the law. "I would like to continue [the Christmas moratorium]," said Judge Patrick J. Sheedy, "but if they are to bring an action against us, we would have no defense." The separation of church and state means the separation of the law from common decency. The ACLU has the satisfaction of having vindicated the great constitutional principle that poor people should be put out on the street on Christmas Day. (*December 1992*)

■ From *The Letters of Martin Buber* (Schocken), this is Abraham Joshua Heschel writing to Buber in Jerusalem. The date is November 25, 1938, and Heschel is in Warsaw, having been forced to flee Frankfurt. "I receive much news from Germany. If only I could respond with deeds! Perhaps this plight will teach us something. . . . Concepts are suddenly regaining their unambiguousness—for everyone. Perhaps we can now bury relativism." Half-a-century later the intellectual masters of clever relativisms, led by Richard Rorty's band of liberal ironists, dance on Heschel's grave, and Buber's. (*February 1993*)

■ Almost twenty-five years ago we were first impressed with the line when attending the funeral of Robert Kennedy at St. Patrick's Cathedral here in New York. In the eulogy, RFK's brother Edward cited a line used by Robert, "Some men see things as they are and say 'Why?' He dreamed things that never were and said 'Why not?'" Now Justice Antonin Scalia comes along and spoils one's appreciation of the statement. Speaking at a Baylor University conference on church-state questions, Scalia noted that the sentiment is lifted from George Bernard Shaw's play *Back to Methuselah*. Shaw's line was: "You see things and you say 'Why?' But I dream things that never were and I say 'Why not?'" It was spoken by the serpent to Eve. *(February 1993)*

■ St. Philip's Catholic Church in San Francisco is apparently one of those places where "the action's at." Jane Gross of the *New York Times* reports on a recent family festival held there, and the point of the report is that, my goodness, there were all kinds of families present—"stepfamilies and foster families, multigenerational families and gay families . . . and other configurations that have yet to be named by social scientists or counted by statisticians." Ms. Gross continues: "Even in this old-fashioned, godly haven, with crucifixions on the walls and children in neat uniforms, the families have changed indelibly but the values have not." Crucifixions on the walls? It seems the action gets a little rough at St. Philip's. The pastor, Father Michael Mealy, draws the lesson to be learned: "There's such a thing as family values, but who's to say who's living up to them?" Certainly not the pastor of St. Philip's. (Crucifixions on the wall reminds us of a Detroit paper that reported some years ago on a Lutheran convention. "The procession was led by a young man carrying a 140-year-old crucifer." But then, why should we expect journalists to know any more about religion than about other matters of consequence?) *(March 1993)*

Sources:

Chapter 1: Tom Burns on John Paul II, *Tablet*, October 22, 1994. On CLUH and Kosher toasters, *Harvard Crimson*, March 12, 1992. On Francis Schaeffer's legacy, *The Rutherford Journal*, March 1993. On contemporary psychiatry, *New York Times*, February 10, 1994. Thanks to Michael C. Tinkler of Atlanta for article on Methodist wedding ceremony for Catholic-Muslin couple, *Atlanta Journal-Constitution*, March 21, 1993. Richard McBrien quoted in *National Catholic Register*, October 6, 1991. Parody titles of hymns in *Christian Challenge*, September 1994.

Chapter 2: Symposium on "The Myth of Racial Progress" in *Christianity Today*, October 4, 1993. Burt Neuborne on the First Amendment's religion clause(s), *Congress Monthly*, November/December 1992. On elimination of religious symbols, *Saint Paul Pioneer Press*, February 11, 1994 (with thanks to Mary Sherry of Burnsville, Minnesota). "Reinhold Niebuhr: Christian Apologist to the Secular World" in *From Marxism to Judaism: Collected Essays of Will Herberg*, edited by David Dalin (Markus Wiener). Judge Carter's sentence reported in *Catholic Standard and Times*, November 11, 1993. On Pettit Linkola and Garret Hardin, *Wall Street Journal*, May 20, 1994. "Politics of the Breast" in *New York Times*, October 2, 1994. Alfred Kazin on Gore Vidal, *The New Republic*, October 5, 1992. Rabbi Gelberman quoted in *New York Times*, February 13, 1993.

Chapter 3: Homosexuality and the Churches: Sr. Ware, *New York Times*, Nov. 4, 1989; Greeley on celibacy, *National Catholic Reporter*, Nov. 10, 1989. Paleoliberal Creed in *Commonweal*, October 23, 1992. On school "Christmas" program in Williamsville, N.Y., *New York Times*, February 26, 1993. On Toledo University, *The Blade*, February 24 and 28, 1992. On Josef Mengele, *New York Times*, February 11, 1992.

Chapter 4: On the Woodstock Center, *Woodstock Report*, March 1990. David Dinkins quote in *Catholic New York*, October 4, 1990. Anti-Defamation League report on anti-Semitism dated November 16, 1992. "An Apology to Native Peoples" reprinted in *Origins*, August 15, 1991. On students preaching hellfire and damnation, *Church & State*, January 1992. Matthew Parris on "coming out" in *Spectator*, 10 August 1991.

Chapter 5: On boys and girls and date rape, *New York Times*, January 2, 1991 and *New York* magazine, January 21, 1991. On Christian handyman, *Milwaukee Journal*, November 24, 1993. Chilstrom interview in *National and International Religion Report*, February 10, 1992, Vol. 6, No. 4. On Kepel's book, *The Revenge of God*, *Economist*, February 26, 1994. Monsignor Byrne on creches and "maternity" in Epiphany Church parish bulletin, June 23, 1991. On ACLU and Christmas evictions, *New York Times*, December 25, 1991. Jane Gross on St. Philip's RC Church, *New York Times*, October 3, 1992.